QUO VADIS?

This book is dedicated to the memory of Fr Justin Coyne CP through whose gentle words and witness I was introduced to a loving God who had counted the hairs on the head of every single child and whose Son Jesus Christ was sent into the world with the express mission of telling us about the unequalled, powerful and underused resource that is and remains the great commandment to love one another.

Mary McAleese

Quo Vadis?
Collegiality in the Code of Canon Law

the columba press

First published in 2012 by
the columba press
55A Spruce Avenue, Stillorgan Industrial Park,
Blackrock, Co. Dublin

Cover by Bill Bolger
Origination by The Columba Press
Printed by MPG Books Group Ltd
ISBN 978 1 85607 786 6

www.columba.ie

Table of Contents

List of Abbreviations   7
Author's Note   9
Acknowledgments   10

Introduction: The Role of Collegiality in Vatican II's *novus habitus mentis* and the 1983 Code of Canon Law   11

1. Towards an Understanding of the Broader Context of Collegiality in the 1983 Code of Canon Law   21

    1.1 Introduction: Terminological Problems   21
    1.2 General Definitions of Collegiality   25
    1.3 Dictionary Definitions   31
    1.4 Weber on Collegiality   34
    1.5 Collegiality and other Christian Churches   34
    1.6 Sources of Meaning and Interpretation   35
    1.7 Scripture   38
    1.8 Tradition   42
    1.9 *Codex Iuris Canonici 1917*   45
    1.10 Other Sources of Meaning   48

2. The Second Vatican Council and Collegiality   55

    2.1 Introduction: Unfinished Business of Vatican I   55
    2.2.1 Vatican II   55
    2.2.2 Within the World: The Broader Setting   56
    2.2.3 Within *Lumen Gentium*: The Broader Setting   61
    2.3 *Lumen Gentium* and Collegiality   63
    2.4 Preliminary Explanatory Note: *Nota Explicativa Praevia*   70
    2.5 Other Vatican II Documents   72
    2.6 Conclusion   77

3. The 1983 Code of Canon Law and Collegiality   79

    3.1 Introduction: The Drafting and Revision Process   79
    3.2 The Apostolic Constitution *Sacrae Disciplinae Leges*   81
    3.3 Collegiality Generally in the 1983 Code of Canon Law   84
    3.4 Procedural Collegiality   86
    3.5.1 Conciliar Collegiality   98
    3.5.2 Collegiality and the People of God   100

3.5.3 Episcopal Collegiality 106
3.6 The Pope 108
3.7 The College of Bishops 113
3.8 The Synod of Bishops 119
3.9 The College of Cardinals 127
3.10 The Roman Curia 132
3.11 *Ad Limina Apostolorum* Visits 136
3.12 Episcopal Councils and Conferences 138
3.13 Diocesan Synods 145
3.14 Conclusion 148

4. Quo Vadis? Whither Collegiality? 153

Sources 162

List of Abbreviations

AAS   *Acta Apostolicae Sedis* – Official gazette of the Holy See through which new laws are promulgated

AG   *Ad Gentes* – Vatican II Decree on the Mission Activity of the Church

ApS   *Apostolos Suos* – Apostolic Letter of Pope John Paul II on the Theological and Juridical nature of Episcopal Conferences (21/5/98)

AS   *Apostolica Sollicitudo* – Apostolic Letter of Pope Paul VI establishing the synod of Bishops for the Universal Church (15/9/65)

CD   *Christus Dominus* – Vatican II Decree on the Pastoral Office of Bishops in the Church

CIC/17   The 1917 Pio-Benedictine Code of Canon Law

CIC   *Codex Iuris Canonici* – 1983 Code of Canon Law

GS   *Gaudium et Spes* – Vatican II Pastoral Constitution on the Church in the Modern World

LEF   *Lex Ecclesiae Fundamentalis* – Unsuccessful attempt post-Vatican II to draft a Church Constitution of Bill of Rights. Some of its provisions were subsumed into the 1983 Code of Canon Law

LG   *Lumen Gentium* – Vatican II Dogmatic Constitution on the Church

Nota   *Nota Explicativa Praevia* – An explanatory note appended to *Lumen Gentium*

PB   *Pastor Bonus* – Apostolic Constitution of Pope John Paul II on reform of the Curia (28/6/88)

PG   *Pastores Gregis* – Post-Synodal Apostolic Exhortation of Pope John Paul II on the ministry of Bishops (16/10/03)

PO   *Presbyterorum Ordinis* – Vatican II Decree on the Ministry and Life of Priests

SC   *Sacrosanctum Concilium* – Vatican II Constitution on the Sacred Liturgy

SDL   *Sacrae Disciplinae Leges* – Apostolic Constitution of Pope John Paul II which instituted the 1983 Code of Canon Law (25/1/83)

UR   *Unitatis Redintegratio* – Vatican II Decree on Ecumenism

Author's Note

This book was written by one of Christ's faithful and is addressed to the Pastors of the Church and to others of Christ's faithful in accordance with Canon 212 of the 1983 Code of Canon Law which reads:

Canon 212 §1. Conscious of their own responsibility, the Christian faithful are bound to follow with Christian obedience those things which the sacred pastors, inasmuch as they represent Christ, declare as teachers of the faith or establish as rulers of the Church.

§2. The Christian faithful are free to make known to the pastors of the Church their needs, especially spiritual ones, and their desires.

§3. According to the knowledge, competence, and prestige which they possess, they have the right and even at times the duty to manifest to the sacred pastors their opinion on matters which pertain to the good of the Church and to make their opinion known to the rest of the Christian faithful, without prejudice to the integrity of faith and morals, with reverence toward their pastors, and attentive to common advantage and the dignity of persons.

Mary McAleese
Rome, Roscommon, Rostrevor
June 2012

Acknowledgments

This book started life as a thesis when I was a part-time student of Canon Law at Milltown Institute, Dublin. I was blessed in my thesis supervisor and lecturer in Canon Law Dr Elizabeth M. Cotter IBVM, whose practical support, encouragement and inspiration made it possible to contemplate such an undertaking and enjoy it. I offer her my abiding gratitude. I also acknowledge with warm thanks the invaluable help I received from the Staff of Milltown Institute, especially Dr David Kelly OSA, Dr Bernadette Flanagan PBVM, Dr Siobhan Larkin HF, Dr Kieran O'Mahony OSA, Dr Michael O'Sullivan SJ, and the Library Staff. I gained very useful advice and insight from the following who commented on my mid-stage presentation, Dr Fintan Gavin, Fr Michael Kilkenny CSSp, and my Canon Law classmates. I am grateful to Fr Michael Hilbert, then Professor of Canon Law at the Gregorian University in Rome, for his encouraging review of the thesis and finally, I thank His Eminence, Cardinal Seán Brady for so promptly and fully answering my factual questions about the Synod of Bishops.

Introduction

The Role of Collegiality in Vatican II's novus habitus mentis and the 1983 Code of Canon Law

> It must be clearly pointed out that this work was brought to completion in an outstandingly collegial spirit; and this not only in regard to the material drafting of the work, but also as regards the very substance of the laws enacted. This note of collegiality, which eminently characterises and distinguishes the process of origin of the present Code, corresponds perfectly with the teaching and the character of the Second Vatican Council. Therefore the Code, not only because of its content but also because of its very origin, manifests the spirit of this Council, in the documents of which the church, the universal 'sacrament of salvation' (cf. *Dogmatic Constitution on the Church, LG,* nos 1, 9, 48) is presented as the people of God and its hierarchical constitution appears based on the College of Bishops united with its Head.[1]

With these words Pope John Paul II introduced the long awaited new Code of Canon Law for the Latin Rite Catholic Church in 1983. This crucial document was designed to give voice and structure to the decisions and spirit of the Second Vatican Council including the Council's deliberations on collegiality. Vatican II was said to have been characterised by an energising spirit of collegiality such as had not been experienced in the church before. It is easy to see why. The entire universal episcopacy, over two thousand bishops (four times more than at Vatican I), had gathered in Rome for the first Council since 1870. Radio and television were there to excite global interest. There

---

1. John Paul II, 25 January 1983, Apostolic Constitution *Sacrae disciplinae leges (SDL)* in *AAS,* 75 (1983), VII–XIV. English translation *The Code of Canon Law,* new rev. Eng. trs prepared by The Canon Law Society of Gt Britain & Ireland in association with The Canon Law Society of Australia & New Zealand and the Canadian Canon Law Society, London, HarperCollins Publishers, 1997, xi–xvi (*CIC*).

were expert theologians, rapporteurs, observers from the laity and other denominations, journalists, and analysts. They came from every continent bringing a rainbow of cultures and languages. Anticipation had been long in the fermenting. Expectations were huge. Interest was enormous. Just to be there must have been intoxicating. There was considerable updating to be done, necessitating widescale deliberation and collaboration, before, during and after the Council.

This collegial forum was not always even-tempered. The atmosphere, for example, during the debate on episcopal conferences was 'not very serene'.[2] Ironically the most bitter debate was over collegiality itself.

Two prime concepts to emerge from Vatican II in summation of the new mentality which was to shape the future of the church, were 'communio' and 'collegiality'. In essence 'communio' characterised the church as the People of God each one of whom, by baptism shares in the three *munera* of Christ's mission of teaching, sanctifying and governing. '*Communio*' signals an active bond of faith which holds the diverse *Christifideles* in union with one another and with the magisterium of the church. It is facilitated within the church in many ways, among them 'collegiality', the word around which issues concerning participation in church governance were discussed.

Commentators differ about the meaning of collegiality. Some argue it is a lost church tradition restored by Vatican II. Others say it is part of the *novus habitus mentis* generated by the Council. For some it is consistent with primatialism and for others it is not. Some see collegiality as a recipe for disunity and schism within the church. Others argue the opposite, while its perceived absence from the Catholic Church is said to be a major barrier to ecumenical dialogue. For some it is about the thoroughgoing quasi-democratisation of the church from the bottom up, while for others it touches only on episcopal collegiality, especially the governance role of the College of Bishops over the universal church.

---

2.   See Guiseppe Alberigo and Joseph A. Komonchak, eds, *History of Vatican II: The Mature Council; Second Period and Intersession: September 1963–September 1964*, vol. III (New York: Leuven: Orbis/Peeters, 2006) [Alberigo and Komonchak, eds, History of Vatican II, Mature Council], 152.

Vatican II's recognition of the College of Bishops' 'supreme and full' power of governance of the universal church contrasted starkly with the then Canon Law of the church set out in the 1917 Pio-Benedictine Code, which recognised only the Pope[3] and Ecumenical Councils[4] as having supreme power. Now thanks to Vatican II it seemed the Pope's personal power had company, summed up loosely, in the phrase 'episcopal collegiality', or in Ghirlanda's words, 'the nature of the juridical structure of the Church is simultaneously collegial and primatial by the will of the Lord himself.'[5] Some have hailed this fresh insight into episcopal collegiality as Vatican II's finest achievement but there was little conciliar guidance and considerable disagreement since, on how it should be realised in practice.

The two main schools of thought are represented by the outstanding church scholars Ladislas Örsy and Gianfranco Ghirlanda (who was involved in the drafting of *CIC*). Örsy sees collegiality as part of the ancient, still-living tradition of the church which is intimately connected with the exercise of episcopal authority in its broadest sense at universal and particular church level. This collegiality has shades of meaning; it is more intense in the case of the College of Bishops and less so in the case of Episcopal Conferences but both are engaged in collegial activity.[6] Ghirlanda says only the formal episcopal collegiality of the full College of Bishops has juridic and theological significance. Other forms of 'collegial' collaboration are little more than *ad hoc*, good will and cooperation.[7]

---

3.   See *Codex Iuris Canonici* 1917, Pii X, *Pontificis maximi iussu digestus Benedicti Papae auctoritate promulgatus*, Typis polyglottis Vaticanis (*CIC/17*), canon (c.) 218 in Edward Peters, ed. *1917 Pio-Benedictine Code in English Translation* (San Francisco: Ignatius Press, 2001). [Peters, ed., *CIC/17*] I have used this translation throughout.

4.   Ibid., c. 228.

5.   Gianfranco Ghirlanda, *Il Diritto Nella Chiesa, Mistero Di Comunione: Compendio Di Diritto Ecclesiale* (Cinisello Balsamo, Milano. Roma: Edizioni Paoline, Editrice Pontificia Università Gregoriana, 1990), 497.

6.   See Ladislas M. Örsy, 'Reflections on the Teaching Authority of the Episcopal Conferences' in Thomas J. Reese, ed., *Episcopal Conferences: Historical, Canonical and Theological Studies* (Washington DC: Georgetown University Press, 1989), 233–52.

7.   See Gianfranco Ghirlanda, 'De Episcoporum Conferentia Deque Exercitio Potestatis Magisterii', *Periodica* 76 (1987): 573–603.

Some commentators differentiate 'effective' from 'affective' collegiality, a view most cogently set out in Pope John Paul II's Apostolic Letter *Apostolos Suos* (*ApS*) where acts of the College of Bishops acting in its entirety are differentiated from acts of individual bishops or groups of bishops, the former being 'effective' and the latter 'affective' collegiality.[8] (No attempt is made to explain the position of the College of Cardinals which is in certain circumstances manifestly 'effective' rather than 'affective' collegiality.)

Pope John Paul II also remarks on the relationship between *communio* and collegiality in the Apostolic Constitution *Pastor bonus* (*PB*).

> When one thinks about this communion, which is the force, as it were, that glues the whole church together, then the hierarchical constitution of the church unfolds and comes into effect. It was endowed by the Lord himself with a primatial and collegial nature at the same time.[9]

Despite such words, Hans Küng believes that Pope John Paul II 'disregarded the collegiality which had been agreed [at Vatican II] and instead celebrated the triumph of his papacy at the cost of the bishops'.[10]

Joseph Ratzinger, among others (writing before he became Pope Benedict XVI), says Vatican II was ambiguous about episcopal collegiality because there was no consensus on its meaning.[11] One school of thought insists that any form of cooperation outside of episcopal collegiality within the College of Bishops, is

8.   See John Paul II, Apostolic letter *Apostolos Suos*, 21 May 1998 in *AAS*, 90 (1998), 641–58, nos. 9–10. English translation from Libreria Editrice Vaticana, www.vatican.va/holy_father/john_paul_ii/motu_proprio/documents/hf_jp-ii_motu-proprio_22071998_apostolos-suos_en.html. [Accessed 01.9.2008.]

9.   John Paul II, Apostolic Constitution *Pastor Bonus*, 28 June 1988, no. 2 in *AAS*, 80 (1988), 177–85. English translation from Libreria Editrice Vaticana, www.vatican.va/holy_father/john_paul_ii/apost_constitutions/documents/hf_jp-ii_apc_19880628_pastor-bonus-index_en.html. [Accessed 01.9 2008.]

10.   Hans Küng, 'The Pope's Contradictions' in *Der Spiegel*, 25 March 2005, English translation in www.spiegel.de/international/spiegel/0,1518,348 471,00.html. [Accessed 10.1.2009.]

11.   See Joseph Ratzinger, *Theological Highlights of Vatican II* (New York: Paulist Press, 1966), 115.

more accurately described as 'co-responsibility' rather than 'collegiality'. Others see any episcopal collegiality outside of an Ecumenical Council as 'affective collegiality' rather than 'effective collegiality', denoting a mood rather than anything juridically significant. Some say the Synod of Bishops is an exercise in episcopal collegiality while others say it falls far short of conciliar collegiality. The word 'collegiality' is also used to describe the post-Conciliar drive towards greater democratisation of governance structures within religious institutes and greater lay involvement in certain areas of church life.

These differing positions illustrate how both '*communio*' and 'collegiality' have been seized by different sides in church debates as code words for either their most feared or their most desired plan for the church's future. As concepts each has an inbuilt elasticity which allows them to be defined just as easily narrowly as widely. Each has a scope for evolution and growth that too rigid an insistence on firm definition could inhibit. Each has a tendency to be talked up aspirationally but rounded down in terms of actual delivery.

In attempting to update the church, Vatican II was dealing with a vast universal institution with a membership of one in six of the global population. The Pope assisted by the Curia formed a monocratic top tier, from which virtually all universal governance flowed. The bishops formed a dispersed second tier concerned mainly with local administrative governance, though a small number served as members of the church's centralised administration known as the Curia. Only at an Ecumenical Council did the general corps of bishops legislate for the universal church.

At the time of Vatican II (and since), no standing forum existed for the regular updating of universal church doctrine and law apart from the Pope himself. The Pope alone could call an Ecumenical Council, a temporary body, which, subject to his overarching approval, had full powers of governance over the universal church. Vatican II was only the third such gathering in four hundred years. It was a legacy body rather than a legislature, dealing in broad brushstrokes rather than fine legalistic detail. There was massive advance preparation and an expectation of further work in its wake, when the process of reception of its many lengthy documents, decisions and deliberations would introduce the Council's *novus habitus mentis* throughout the entire church.

With no interim graduated process of self-updating outside of papal decrees, Ecumenical Councils had in the past often produced a lurching effect with the ever-present threat of schism in the face of what appeared to be sudden change. The shadow of controversy lingered long over many previous Councils so Vatican II demanded great delicacy.

It was never going to be easy to find practical ways of including in day to day universal church governance, several thousand highly dispersed bishops and it was going to be even more difficult, to find meaningful ways of facilitating the participation of all the faithful in church governance. Without being structurally prescriptive, the Council indicated that it wanted the post-conciliar church to explore pathways to both while at the same time maintaining the integrity of papal authority and church unity. The sheer scale of such an undertaking cannot be overestimated while the timescale, to judge by the progress on both fronts, has been seriously underestimated. The word 'collegiality' became a flag of verbal convenience under which much post-conciliar discussion of this exploration has taken place.

Those who drafted the new Code of Canon Law had to work with imperfect Council outcomes. They had to update the law in line with conciliar innovations, yet reconcile it with tradition. They had to take account of the College of Bishops' role in shared governance yet leave primatialism intact. They had to provide canonically for conciliar collegiality without clear guidance as to its limits. Just as the Council struggled with these dilemmas, so too did the Code Commission which was charged with the task of drafting the new Code when the Council ended. Ultimately collegiality's development was left almost entirely at the discretion of the Pope.

Within the relevant church documents, the 1983 Code included, there is considerable variation in both the contexts and meanings ascribed to collegiality and words associated with it, like 'college', 'collegial' and 'collegiate'. Sometimes these words are used in a juridically narrow, technical way and sometimes they are used to describe broader ecclesiological concepts.

However even where used in a legalistic or technical way they convey attitudes about the nature of activity that can properly and juridically be described as collegial and in so doing they help inform the debate on the wider sphere of collegiality.

Reflecting on developments since Vatican II, Örsy cautions against impatience, seeing the Conciliar legacy regarding collegiality, as being made manifest over centuries rather than decades, 'a slow burn' and an evolutionary process of revelation of Divine will.[12] Lash, by contrast suggests that the shutters may be coming down on Vatican II, which has failed to live up to its promises and expectations.[13] Yet others see no problem. Cardinal José Saraiva Martins, Prefect of the Congregation for the Causes of Saints was of that opinion when interviewed during the 2001 Synod of Bishops. 'Collegiality is by now a very pacific theme, agreed upon by all, also in practice. It can be emphasised, it can be reformulated, but in its essence collegiality is already in vigour in the church.'[14]

Muraille asserts that having placed the Pope firmly within and not apart from the People of God and within and not apart from the Episcopal College, though as its head, the Council did no more than set out the basic principles on which the subsequent development of effective ecclesiastical (and not exclusively episcopal) collegiality was to be built in the post-conciliar era.[15] Similarly, Ratzinger claims that the 'concept of collegiality, besides the office of unity which pertains to the Pope, signifies an element of variety and adaptability that basically belongs to the structure of the church but may be actuated in many ways'.[16]

---

12. See Ladislas M. Örsy, 'Peter and Paul Seminar: The Unfinished Work of Collegiality', *Woodstock Report*, Spring, no. 81 (2005).
13. See Nicholas Lash, 'Could the Shutters yet Come Down?', *The Tablet*, 24 January (2009): 13.
14. See John L. Allen Jr, 'Collegiality vs. Centralization Dominates Synod', *National Catholic Reporter*, 12 October 2001, www.natcath.org/NCR_Online/archives2/2001d/101201/101201f.html. [Accessed 06.5.2009.]
15. See Phillipe Muraille, 'The Logic of Vatican Council II' in José De Broucker, *The Suenens Dossier: The Case for Collegiality* (Notre Dame, Indiana: Fides, 1970), 126.
16. Joseph Ratzinger, 'The Pastoral Implications of Episcopal Collegiality', *Concilium*, 1 (1964): 64.

The 1983 Code was, according to *SDL*, to manifest and give visible expression to the Council's collegial spirit and doctrine 'in the very substance of the laws enacted'. In this study I intend to examine the provision made in *CIC* for collegiality and to distil the scholarly commentaries and analyses which shed light on the expectations and experience of collegiality within the Latin Rite Catholic Church. I hope to be able to explain the history, meaning and development of collegiality, describe the doctrine, delineate the various models of collegiality found in *CIC* and assess whether and to what extent they have met or are likely to meet expectations. I hope to be able to ascertain whether colleg - iality is a promise that was fulfilled or not. Was it a leavening spirit, a long-term infusion of a *novus habitus mentis* or is it too soon to tell? Was it a new idea at all? Is it part of the lived reality of church life and if it is, what is it and where can it be found?

The study will necessarily examine episcopal collegiality, a major focus of Vatican II and of ongoing scholarly interest from inside and outside the church. It is intimately connected to the question of church governance. However episcopal collegiality is only one of a number of models of so-called collegial practice within the church and in particular within *CIC*. There is considerable guidance on general collegial procedures within *CIC*'s section on General Norms, most of which existed before Vatican II. Post Vatican II saw the development of what have been described as collegial governance structures within religious institutes, notably within general chapters.[17] The Post Synodal Apostolic Exhortation *Pastores gregis* (*PG*) describes as greenshoot 'affective collegiality'[18] national, regional, international and supranational episcopal conferences, particular councils, *ad limina* visits, missionary activity, the work of the Curia and Synods.[19] However *PG*, echoing Ghirlanda, also sees the

---

17.   See Elizabeth M. Cotter, *The General Chapter in a Religious Institute: With Particular Reference to IBVM Loreto Branch* (Bern: Peter Lang, 2008) [Elizabeth M. Cotter, General Chapter].

18.   See John Paul II, Apostolic Exhortation *Pastores Gregis* (16 October 2004), no. 8 in *AAS* 96, 2004, 825–924.

19.   See Myriam Wijlens, 'Exercising Collegiality in a Supranational or Continental Institution Such as the FABC, CCEE and COMECE,' *The Jurist*, 64 (2004): 168–204.

expression 'affective collegiality' as a loose non-juridic term for forms of ecclesial collaboration which fall outside the scope of the more juridic term 'full' or 'effective' collegiality which applies, he believes, only to the College of Bishops.

Anchoring this study in the canonical provision for collegiality, I hope to be able to describe the journey into collegiality since Vatican II.

CHAPTER ONE

Towards an Understanding of the Broader Context of Collegiality in the 1983 Code of Canon Law

1.1 Introduction: Terminological Problems

This study looks at how the 1983 Code of Canon Law (*CIC*) deals with collegiality. What does the word 'collegiality' (and related words) mean in Canon Law? When words are used as terms of legal art, definitions based on colloquial use, or set in the context of special pleading in debates, or used in the abstract, are not necessarily adequate or correct. *CIC* c. 17 warns that ecclesiastical laws must be understood in the light of their text and context and so these too will inevitably shape the meaning to be properly ascribed to certain words.

A drawback to any study of ecclesial collegiality is the extent to which the word 'collegiality' itself and related words are used without definition or with inconsistent and conflicting meanings in significant church documents including the key document to understanding episcopal collegiality, the Dogmatic Constitution on the Church, *Lumen Gentium* (*LG*)[1] and *CIC* itself. The same lack of definition and inconsistency are to be found in many of the academic, theological or canonical publications which treat of collegiality. They also appear in *CIC/17* (that is the 1917 Pio-Benedictine Code).

In an audience with Bishop Charue of Namur during Vatican II, Pope Paul VI is reported to have said that collegiality 'is beyond doubt but what power does it have?'[2] That sentence summarises both the dilemma at the heart of and the eventual outcome of the conciliar debate on collegiality. The question left

---

1. See Second Vatican Council, Dogmatic Constitution on the Church *Lumen Gentium*, 22 November 1964 in *AAS*, 57 (1964), 5–75 (*LG*).
2. Alberigo and Komonchak, eds, *History of Vatican II: Mature Council*, 423.

hanging by Pope Paul VI was not answered by *CIC* but rather
imported into it for the Code was not designed to settle such a
question. It was, at the time of the Council, a question posed
largely in relation to episcopal collegiality but not so exclusively
as to deaden any arguments for a collegiality, whatever its juridical status, which reached beyond the sphere of the episcopal.

The breadth of conflicting views on the meaning and scope
of collegiality is very evident both in the conciliar schema and
conciliar debates where eventual harmonisation proved elusive.
Similar problems are evident in the preparatory documents for
CIC. Conciliar difficulties with episcopal collegiality are however
only part of the story. Unsatisfactory though both Council and
CIC may be on that subject, the words 'college', 'collegial' and
'collegiate' and the inference of collegiality arise in other contexts in *LG* and other church documents and in *CIC*. In so doing
they open up other chapters in the narrative on collegiality in
CIC with a variety of contexts, meanings and juridic outcomes.
They also add greatly to the confusion.

Allowing that the official language of *CIC* is Latin and that
English translations vary (e.g. 'collegial' and 'collegiate' are used
interchangeably in some circumstances), the words 'collegial',[3]
'collegially'[4] or 'collegiality'[5] appear twenty-nine times in the
Code and its introductory documentation, that is to say both
SDL and the preface to the Latin edition of *CIC*. The introductory
documents account for ten of the references and for the two sole
references to 'collegiality'. The word 'college/s'[6] appears some
eighty-five times in a wide variety of contexts. The word 'collegiate'[7] also appears on at least eleven and arguably fourteen
occasions depending on which translation is used. The words

---

3.   See *SDL,* Latin text Preface and canons (cc.) 115, 119, 120, 333, 337, 341,
        353, 503, 505, 508, 509.

4.   See *SDL,* and cc. 140, 337, 349, 443, 699, 1425 and 1441.

5.   See *SDL.*

6.   See *SDL* and cc. 115, 127, 135, 158, 160, 165, 166, 169, 173, 174, 175, 176, 177,
        182, 183, 264, 272, 330, 331, 336, 337, 339, 341, 349, 350, 351, 352, 359, 375,
        377, 382, 404, 413, 419, 421, 422, 430, 485, 494, 501, 502, 503, 557, 749, 752,
        753, 754, 755, 756, 782, 833, 1018, 1277, 1292, 1372, 1421, 1428, 1505 and
        1609.

7.   See cc. 491, 1425, 1426, 1428, 1449, 1455, 1505, 1609, 1610 and 1612.

'collaborate'[8] and 'cooperate'[9] (or variants of them) which also appear some fifteen times and twenty-nine respectively, may in a number of instances, shed light on the nature of and limits on collegial activity especially vis-à-vis 'co-responsibility'. This latter concept is sometimes used to differentiate between episcopal collegiality and other forms of cooperative or consultative endeavour within the church especially where they occur at sub-Episcopal College level. There are important church documents which deal with collegiality where neither the word itself nor any related term is used. Similarly there are canons in *CIC*, of fundamental importance to collegiality which make no mention of the word or related terms at all.

The rules for interpreting ecclesiastical laws are set out in *CIC* (cc. 16–22). They tell us that such laws are to be understood 'in accord with the proper meaning of the words considered in their text and context' (c. 17). Where the meaning remains in doubt 'there must be recourse to parallel places [...] to the purpose and circumstance of the law and to the mind of the Legislator' (c. 17). Archbishop Burke of St Louis observes that the

> [...] correct understanding and right applications of the canons of Church discipline depend upon knowledge of the mind of the Legislator. The rules of canonical interpretation [...] require a diligent study of the evolution of the text of the law, taking care to understand the precise meaning of terms in the context from which they have been drawn to articulate the Church's discipline.[10]

SDL sets out another fundamental rule of interpretation when it says that in case of doubt, one refers to the Council.[11] *CIC/17* though largely repealed by the new Code still forms part of the canonical tradition and practice of the church and may have a continuing interpretive relevance where the 'old law is embedded in the canons'.[12]

---

8.   See *SDL* for references to collaborate, collaborated, collaboration and collaborators, also cc. 364, 652, 796, 1446 (collaborate) cc. 528 and 825 (collaboration).

9.   See *SDL* for references to cooperation, also cc. 129, 208, 328, 356, 529, 652, 713, 759, 796 (cooperate), cc. 1041 (cooperated), cc. 311, 822 (cooperating) and cc. 275, 276, 369, 434, 519, 680, 782, 820, 1090 and 1096 (cooperation).

10. Eduardus N. Peters, *Incrementa in Progressu: 1983 Codicis Iuris Canonici*, Gratianus (Montreal: Wilson & Lafleur, 2005), foreword.

11. See *SDL*.

12. See Alberigo and Komonchak, eds, *History of Vatican II: Mature Council*, 423.

These interpretative rules do not always lead to crystal clarity for as some commentators have noted words like 'college', 'collegial', 'collegially' and 'collegiality' are consistently used inconsistently in ecclesiastical law, sometimes in narrow technical ways and sometimes in much broader abstract ways. They are often used in these different ways in the same document. *LG* is a case in point as is *SDL* and *CIC* itself.

According to Herranz the words 'collegial' and 'collegiality' are often used 'with little juridical precision'[13] when speaking of the College of Bishops. The same can be said for the word 'college', which is undefined in *CIC* and used in many different senses and with very different canonical consequences. Even where *CIC* attaches a strict juridic meaning to the word 'college' in a particular set of circumstances, this may or may not be the same as the 'strict juridic meaning' accorded to the same word in the Preliminary Explanatory Note (*Nota Explicative Praevia* is *Nota*) in *LG*.[14] The *Nota* also says that such a strict juridic meaning does not apply to the College of Bishops.

Ratzinger says '*collegium*' was first applied to bishops as far back as the third century but other words were also used, such as '*ordo*' or '*corpus*' or '*fraternitas*', indicating that no single concept could fully describe the communal nature of the episcopal office.[15] Indeed, the word 'college' was not used to describe the universal body of bishops in *CIC/17*.

A 'collegial juridic person' (a specific and defined legal entity within *CIC*), is capable of placing 'collegial acts' which arise from the deliberative votes of members of the juridic person. However other groups, which are not collegial juridic persons, are sometimes described as 'acting collegially' by which is meant something quite different from the collegial acts of a collegial juridic person.

The word 'collegiality' itself does not appear in *CIC* but only in *SDL*. There, it is undefined but used in different ways. Firstly it is used colloquially to describe the collaborative working

---

13.   Ibid., 144.
14.   See Flannery, 93–5.
15.   See Ratzinger, 'The Pastoral Implications of Episcopal Collegiality', 39–67.

mood of those involved in the drafting of *CIC*. Secondly and more juridico/technically it describes the laborious consultative process by which *CIC* was drafted. Thirdly, also of juridical significance, it situates collegiality as part of the church doctrine of '*communio*'.

Any discussion of collegiality within *CIC* needs to explore both the strict juridic and more abstract use of these terms, for each sets certain very divergent predictors in terms of consequences. Since both text and context are important in interpreting *CIC*'s provisions, I turn first to the broader context in which the concept of collegiality is set, for general guidance and background as to its meaning.

1.2 General Definitions of Collegiality

At its simplest, the idea of collegiality is rooted, no matter how vaguely, in the notion of a college. It suggests a gathering of individuals into a common association or grouping ring-fenced in some identifiable way. In common parlance it often covers relationships within a school or university community, embracing teachers, ancillary staff and students where relationships may be quite hierarchical and authority roles are highly differentiated. Many church documents concerning education use it in this way with no insinuation of equality of status among college members or of entitlement to deliberative votes which could directly govern the college. Used colloquially it also often describes certain stable groups such as professions or associations of people with a specific common denominator, where there may or may not be equal status among members but where it would not be uncommon to find the membership engaged in decision making processes as of right. Church documents, including *CIC* use it in both such contexts and others.

In *CIC* the term 'collegial' is used often but not always where it has a relatively precise meaning, generally associated with the acts of a juridic aggregate of persons, a distinctive legal entity in its own right, members of which make decisions together although there is no requirement of equality of status among members. It is the shared making of decisions that identifies the entity as collegial and differentiates it from a non-collegial jur - idic person.

'Collegial' and 'collegiality' are often used colloquially and canonically to cover a range of relationships deriving from con-joint as opposed to individual activity, such as collaboration, co-operation, consultation or co-responsibility. In such cases there may not be any clearly delineated group character or identity or there may be a number of identifiable groups whose external relations with each other may be described loosely as collegial over and against combative or fraught. The word has even been used to describe, as a 'collegial choice', the decision of Pope Benedict XVI to remit, in January 2009, the excommunication of four bishops of the schismatic Society of St Pius X, among whom was a Bishop Williamson, a controversial Holocaust denier.[16] By contrast Willey claims the decision was made personally by the Pope[17] and Pabel says this decision 'is yet another instance of the collapse of collegiality'.[18]

In the sphere of social science, 'collegiality' has been used to denote organisational models which are neither bureaucratic nor monocratic in nature and in which the exercise of power is tempered by being collegially diffused to some extent or other. It may lead to greater democratisation within organisations but Weber remarks that collegiality is not necessarily a harbinger of democracy and sits just as easily with hierarchical structures.[19] Lakeland says much the same about collegiality within the Church.

> While on the surface it sounds a clear democratising note, drawing the bishops together into a greater responsibility for the governance of the church, it is also susceptible to a more conservative turn. In this interpretation, the bishops' role in ecclesial governance is little more than their expression of solidarity with the papal voice.[20]

---

16.   See Editorial, *L'Osservatore Romano*, 26–7 January 2009.
17.   See David Willey, 'A Gaffe Too Far', *The Tablet*, 7 February (2009): 4.
18.   Hilmar M. Pabel, 'Vatican Counsel', *The Tablet*, 21 February (2009): 11.
19.   See Max Weber, *Economy and Society: An Outline of Interpretive Sociology*, ed. Claus Wittich and Ephraim Fischoff Guenther Roth (Berkeley: University of California Press, 1978), 273.
20.   Paul Lakeland, 'John Paul II and Collegiality' in Gerard Mannion, *The Vision of John Paul II: Assessing his Thought and Influence* (Collegeville, Minn: Liturgical Press, 2008), 185.

The apostles are often described as a 'college'. The Vatican II decree on the Church's Missionary Activity *Ad Gentes* refers to 'the body of bishops which succeeds the college of the apostles'.[21] As we will see later in looking at *CIC*'s provisions the word 'college' is used to cover the non-strictly juridic College of Bishops (c. 336), the 'special' College of Cardinals (c. 349), College of Consultors (c. 502), College of Judges (cc. 1425 and 1426), judicial colleges, (c. 135) college of priests (c. 503), college of students (c. 264), college of teachers (c. 264), colleges of equals, colleges of members who are not equals, colleges which can place collegial acts, colleges which cannot place collegial acts, collegial acts which are strictly juridic and collegial acts which are not and colleges as opposed to groups, though clearly a college is a particular species of group. There are collegiate churches, collegial acts, things or processes which must be done collegially to be valid and there are actions, processes and juridic persons which are described as non-collegial. The fact that *CIC* accommodates all these uses may be the only single common denominator they share, for the more one searches for commonality the more elusive it seems.

Episcopal collegiality produced the most divisive conciliar debate. The outcome was ambiguous definitions of both a 'college' and 'collegiality' in *LG* and the *Nota*. Still, the adoption by the Vatican Council of the principle of episcopal collegiality is regarded as one of its prime achievements. Muraille observes that the Council avoided being prescriptive about the relationship between the Pope and the episcopal college and instead gave 'only the principles for a solution'.[22]

If the Second Vatican Council was vague regarding episcopal collegiality it was more obscure still on the broader application of the principle of collegiality throughout the church. Collegiality at sub-episcopal college level remained unclear though provision was made for a number of developments that tilted towards greater collegiality / co-responsibility, such as the

---

21.   See Vatican II, Decree on the Church's Missionary Activity *Ad Gentes Divinitus* (7 December 1965) in *AAS*, 58 (1966), 947–90, no. 38 in Flannery, 491.

22.   See José De Broucker, *The Suenens Dossier: The Case for Collegiality*, 126.

Synod of Bishops, obligatory episcopal conferences and greater
lay cooperation at parish and diocesan level or as experts in certain prescribed areas. These would all eventually be translated
into *CIC* and in their concrete realisation would begin to develop a life of their own. Whether these developments belong to the
conciliar principle of collegiality or to a different sphere entirely
is a subject of ongoing debate. Some commentators insist
'collegiality' applies only to episcopal collegiality and everything else is 'co-responsibility'. Cardinal Carli says episcopal
conferences lack the three elements necessary for episcopal collegiality.

1. Involvement of the entire college of bishops.
2. Participation of the Pope
3. Matters before them must concern the universal church.[23]

Komonchak insists that Vatican II saw episcopal conferences
as 'conjoint'[24] rather than collegial and since their immediate
purpose is practical and local, they cannot be considered colleg -
ial. This gives a clear, albeit horizontal scope to collegiality
drawing a firm line below which the term 'collegiality' does not
apply. It is a view supported by *ApS* and *PG* to some extent in
their differentiation between affective collegiality and effective
collegiality. Such views may help us to understand what collegiality is not but may still not explain what collegiality is, even
when practised within that restricted sphere.

Gröte claims collegiality 'permeates church life … no other
institution on this earth produces collegiality to this extent and
degree. But it would be ungovernable without hierarchicalism'.[25] Such a view, if unrefined, could leave us in danger of seeing every place within the church where two or more are gathered as an exercise of the principle of collegiality, reducing the
principle to such a level of vacuousness as to make one wonder
why it engendered such fiery passion at the Council. Gröte's

---

23.   See Alberigo and Komonchak, eds, *History of Vatican II: Mature Council*, 126.
24.   See Joseph A. Komonchak 'Introduction: Episcopal Conferences under
        Criticism' in Thomas J. Reese, ed., *Episcopal Conferences: Historical,
        Canonical and Theological Studies*, 18.
25.   See Heiner Gröte, 'The Catholic Conception of Collegiality from a
        European Reformed Perspective', *Concilium*, 4 (1990): 63.

subsequent definition of collegiality brings us back to the core conciliar debate, for along with respect for the leader he argues that collegiality assumes equality of membership and active participation in decision making.[26] William Sexton on the other hand observes that hierarchies generally believe lower ranks participate in decision making much more than they actually do.[27]

Since Vatican II there have been ongoing debates about both episcopal collegiality and collegiality/collaboration/co-responsibility at regional, national, diocesan and parish level, in other words among all the People of God as defined by *LG*. In the case of the latter, commentators sometimes talk more of a spirit of collegiality observable in informal cooperation and collaboration rather than juridically structured collegiality with precise rights and clearly scoped juridical/legal roles. It is certainly neater and easier (whatever about theologically or canonically sound) to see this sub-episcopal college activity, as more correctly belonging to a much wider area of co-responsibility which is shared by all the faithful. It allows for a capacious area of generalised conjoint activity throughout the church, known as co-responsibility which has conciliar roots. A distinctive subcategory of co-responsibility would be the collegiality of the College of Bishops and it is to that sphere alone that the juridic conciliar principle of collegiality would apply. Those who advocate this interpretation see the more abstract use of the term 'collegiality' outside of the College of Bishops, as something of a danger in terms of seeding juridic confusion at best, or disunity at worst.[28]

Clifford says collegiality and conciliarism are associated and that there needs to be a new understanding of papal primacy in line with the changes sought by the majority at Vatican II where although papal primacy was re-affirmed, the supreme power of the College of Bishops was acknowledged for the first time. Clifford is not just interested though in the exercise of episcopal

26.   See ibid., 54.
27.   See William Sexton, 'Collegiality and Subsidiarity', *Review for Religious*, November (1970): 857–64.
28.   See Angel Marzoa, Jorge Miras, and Rafael Rodriguez-Ocana, eds, *Exegetical Commentary on the Code of Canon Law*, 5 vols, vol. 1 (Montreal: Wilson & Lafleur, 2004) [Exegetical Commentary, 144].

collegiality. She believes the collegial principle 'calls for all levels of the church to share in concern and responsibility for the total life of the church'.[29] Collegiality to her does not mean simply consultation. She complains that decades after the Council collegiality still depends entirely on initiation by the Pope, there are no fixed structures which develop collegiality on a standing basis and the conciliar vision of collegiality still awaits implementation.

The broader view of conciliar collegiality has developed most coherently within religious institutes, where as Cotter establishes, in the process of reception of the *novus habitus mentis* of the Council, there has been a clear move away from autocratic governance structures towards (the recovery of historically normative) collegially participative, even democratic structures.[30]

Örsy argues for a theology of collegiality which embraces the entire People of God in *communio* while Küng envisages a collegiality of all the faithful, arising from baptism which leads inexorably to 'a dissolution of that authoritarian one-man rule'.[31] Tierney asserts that such a collegiality existed in the church from the days of the apostles and for many centuries thereafter.[32]

In summary, the word 'collegiality' and its related words have been used in such a multiplicity of ways that to quote Ratzinger (though in a different context), 'there exists the dangerous temptation to pick out the solutions that appear most congenial'.[33]

29.   See Catherine Clifford, 'Emerging Consensus on Collegiality and Catholic Ecumenical Responsibility', *The Jurist*, 64 (2004): 332–60.

30.   See Elizabeth M. Cotter, *General Chapter*, 64.

31.   See Hans Küng, *Reforming the Church Today: Keeping Hope Alive*, trs P. Heinegg with F. McDonagh et al. (New York: The Crossroad Publishing Company, 1990), 89.

32.   See Brian Tierney, 'Church Law and Alternative Structures. A Medievalist Perspective' in Francis Oakley and Bruce Russett, eds, *Governance, Accountability, and the Future of the Catholic Church* (New York: Continuum, 2004), 49–61.

33.   Ratzinger, Joseph Cardinal, *Called to Communion: Understanding the Church Today*, trs Adrian Walker (San Francisco: Ignatius Press, 1991), 14.

1.3 Dictionary Definitions

Most searches for meaning predictably include a trawl through
the relevant dictionaries. The *Shorter Oxford English Dictionary*
defines collegiality as 'the relationship of, or appropriate to, colleagues: spec. joint responsibility [especially] of Roman Catholic
Bishops in church governance.'[34]

The concept of a collegial forum as one in which members
exercise 'joint responsibility' for governance is qualitatively different from one where they collaborate, are consulted, engage in
conjoint activity, share common facilities or simply behave in an
appropriately collegial spirit to one another. This last has more
to do with what *LG* calls 'the bond of unity, charity and peace'
which unites the members of the College of Bishops with each
other and with the Pope.[35] Yet this definition, of 'collegiality'
embraces a broad spectrum. It is capable of covering many other
areas of Church life besides the College of Bishops, for example
the College of Cardinals (c. 349), episcopal conferences (c. 455),
Synods of Bishops (c. 343), diocesan synods (c. 460), religious institutes (c. 607), presbyteral councils (c. 495), juridic persons (c.
113) and arguably even the 'People of God' (c. 204). It is not expressly prescriptive as to whether collegiality involves a role in
decision taking, though 'joint responsibility' would seem to
imply it does. The same dictionary defines a '*collegium*' as 'an
advisory or administrative board.'[36] and a 'college' as among
other things, an

> ... association, partnership; an organised body of people per-
> forming certain common functions and sharing certain privi-
> leges. An assemblage or company of individuals. A reunion, a
> meeting of companions. A community of clergy living together
> on a foundation for religious service ...[37]

In Burke's *Dictionary of Canon Law*, a 'college' is defined as a

> ... public juridical person: a body where all are equal and the
> Head of the College is understood to be the first among equals;

---

34. Lesley Brown, ed., *New Shorter Oxford English Dictionary* (Oxford: Clar-
     endon Press, 1993), 440.

35. See Flannery, 29.

36. Brown, *New Shorter Oxford English Dictionary*, 440.

37. Ibid., 439.

it functions as one. Its decisions are binding upon all members
... a college is not a council. There is no such thing as a college
without its Head.[38]

The reference to 'Its decisions' points towards a decision
making process involving the entire membership including the
Head. Burke's later definition of a 'collegial act' says 'it is of the
essence of a juridic person that all its members participate in the
decision making in accordance with the norm of law, whether
that law is universal or particular or statutory.'[39] The word
'participate' is of course qualified by the phrase 'in accordance
with the norm of law'. Some form of participation by all the
members is implied and given the term 'equals' used in the definition of 'college' and the assertion that 'it functions as one,' it
implies that a collegial participative process goes beyond simple
passivity of the membership or autocracy of the Head.

The emphasis on members' equality and participation in decision making is absent from Burke's definition of the College of
Bishops.

> That College composed of the bishops of the world in union
> with its Head (and never without its Head) and subject to him as
> the supreme and full power over the universal church. In the
> College the Head preserves intact his function as Vicar of Christ
> and pastor of the universal church. It only occasionally engages
> in strictly collegial activity and then only with the consent of its
> Head.[40]

This is as much a definition of a hierarchical/monarchical structure as a collegial structure for the only status of the members
which is emphasised in the fact that they are 'subject' to their
Head. 'Strictly collegial activity' is the exception rather than
the rule and even then is only permissible with the consent of
the Head, who at all times, not just has but is 'the supreme
and full power over the universal church'. This is quite some
distance from the 'joint responsibility' for governance mentioned
above in the *Shorter Oxford Dictionary* and from the conciliar

---

38.   John Burke, *A Dictionary of Canon Law* (Akure, Nigeria: Don Bosco publi-
       cations, 2004), 78.

39.   Ibid., 79.

40.   Ibid., 78.

acknowledgment of the College of Bishops' full and supreme power of governance. It comes close (like *PG*) to a juridical definition of episcopal collegiality which is exhausted by partic- ipation in Ecumenical Councils. Since those with a deliberative vote at the First and Second Vatican Councils were a wider constituency than simply the College of Bishops, including as they did, non-bishop Cardinals as well as bishops not yet consecrated, one wonders when precisely, if ever, the College of Bishops has acted (or been allowed to act) exclusively as the College of Bishops.

In Stelten's *Dictionary of Ecclesiastical Latin* a *Collegialis actus* is tightly defined as 'collegial act; a decision reached by all the delegates of a college together, arrived at by an absolute majori- ty vote'.[41] The *episcopale collegium* is defined somewhat tersely as 'Episcopal College; all the bishops of the world, of whom the Supreme Pontiff is the Head.'[42] While *collegialis* is defined as 'collegial; acting together' there is no explanation of what that means in the context of the Episcopal College.

The *New Dictionary of Theology* provides this intriguing defin- ition:

> Collegiality as both a doctrine and an attitude is one of the distinctive features of the ecclesiology of Vatican II. In the strict sense collegiality refers to the doctrine that all bishops, by virtue of their episcopal consecration and their hierarchical commu- nion among themselves and with the head of the college, the Pope, have a corporate responsibility for the unity of the faith and of communion in the universal church. [The] spirit of colle- giality can also be reflected in the local church or diocese through presbyteral and pastoral councils.[43]

The Encyclopaedic Dictionary of Roman Law defines '*collegia*' as 'Associations of both private and public character, unions of dif- ferent kinds and for different purposes (professional, cultural, charitable, religious). [...] Originally they had (probably since the twelve tables) the right to assembly, they were permitted to

---

41.   Leo F. Stelten, *Dictionary of Ecclesiastical Latin: With an Appendix of Latin Expressions Defined and Clarified (Peabody, Mass:* Hendrickson, 1995), 304.

42.   Ibid., 305.

43.   Joseph A. Komonchak, Mary Collins, and Dermot A. Lane, *The New Dictionary of Theology* (Collegeville, Minn.: Liturgical Press, 1990), 210.

issue statutes concerning their organisation, activity and the
rights and duties of their members.'[44]

1.4 Weber on Collegiality

Social scientist, Max Weber sees collegiality as essentially a limit
on the exercise of authority. He describes it as taking a wide variety of forms, from advisory collegial bodies whose advice may
or may not temper the power of the chief, to bodies each of
whose members have an absolute power of veto on the acts of a
chief. He remarks that collegiality is 'in no sense specifically democratic' but it 'favours greater thoroughness in the weighing
of administrative decisions'.[45] This may or may not always be a
desirable thing for he warns: 'Collegiality almost inevitably involves obstacles to precise, clear and above all rapid decisions.'
Rapid decision making is however relatively rare in the church
and so it should have considerable scope for slower more deliberative collegial structures though some might see one plenary
meeting per century of an institution's top governing echelon as
rather too slow. Weber also notes the tendency over time for the
lead member of collegial bodies 'to become substantively and
even formally pre-eminent. This is true of the position of the
bishops and the Pope in the church ...'[46]

1.5 Collegiality and other Christian Churches

Christian churches have long differed over collegiality. The 2005
report of the Faith and Order Commission of the World
Community of Churches is of interest for the breadth of its description of collegiality and its acknowledgment of the role that
can be played by delegated or representational collegiality.

> Collegiality refers to the corporate, representative exercise in the
> areas of leadership, consultation, discernment, and decision
> making. Collegiality entails the personal and relational nature
> of leadership and authority. Collegiality is at work wherever
> those entrusted with oversight gather, discern, speak and act as

---

44.   Adolf Berger, *Encyclopaedic Dictionary of Roman Law: New Series*
      (Philadephpia: The American Philosophical Society, 1953), vol. 43, Part 2,
      195.

45.   See Weber, *Economy and Society*, 276.

46.   Ibid., 277.

one on behalf of the whole church. This implies leading the church by means of the wisdom gained by corporate prayer, study and reflection, drawing on scripture, tradition and reason – the wisdom and experience of all church communities throughout the ages. Sustaining collegiality involves preventing premature closure of debate, ensuring that different voices are heard, listening to expert opinion and drawing on appropriate sources of scholarship … Speaking collegially can mean reflecting back to the community the legitimate diversity that exists within the life of the church.[47]

1.6 Sources of Meaning and Interpretation

To someone like me, trained as a civil lawyer in the Common Law tradition, a search for legal meaning generally involves primary and secondary sources. Primary sources are found in the natural meaning of the text of the law itself, in any formal statutory definitions set out in the relevant law or in similar laws and in judicial precedent ascertained from learned judgments set out in published case law. Secondary sources may be found in governmental reports, expert commentaries, *travaux preparatoires*, unpublished judgments as well as scholarly articles and books. It is rare, indeed counter-intuitive in the Common Law tradition, to examine the innards of the drafting processes through which a piece of legislation has gone, in order to analyse the subtle textual changes prior to finalisation. Such information is not generally available to the public, though once draft legislation reaches parliament from the parliamentary office responsible for drafting, all subsequent debates and amendments are published in the public domain.

In Canon Law, the research pathway has some but not always exact parallels with civil law. It has noteworthy differences especially the significance attached, by canonists, to the textual changes made over the course of the drafting process. Nor is the demarcation between primary and secondary sources always as clear in Canon Law as it is in Civil Law where scholarly interpretations may be at best influential but have no authoritative

---

47. Faith and Order Commission of the World Council of Churches, Paper No. 198, *The Nature and Mission of the Church: A Stage on the Way to a Common Statement* (December 2005), par. 97.

weight. The 'canonical tradition' (now expressed in *CIC* c. 16) confers on the Legislator, primary interpretative authority and inclines more to informal praxis rather than to precedent, but, is said to hold private interpretations of Canon Law by scholars in 'high regard'.[48] In a complex and secretive system that lacks any regular standing means of self-updating or public scrutiny, like a senate, parliament or court, this system confers considerable influence on both scholars and the bureaucracy that supports the 'Legislator' (a term used in a sense very different from the secular world and which in particular does not involve the separation of legislative, executive and judicial powers, the very *sine qua non* of a democracy). It is also less than conducive to legal certainty. This point was given no little prominence in the 2009 report of the Irish civil Commission of Enquiry into the handling of clerical child abuse in the Dublin Archdiocese when it accepted as 'truthful and accurate' the evidence of the Dublin Archdiocese judicial vicar who 'did not shrink from painting a picture on occasion of chaos and confusion within the archdiocese and between the archdiocese and Rome'.[49]

Herwi Rikhof, in searching for the meaning of 'collegiality' in *LG*, acknowledges that 'the text itself must be primary' but suggests that 'intention and prehistory are not superfluous to a good understanding of the text. They can offer help in explaining characteristics or peculiarities of the text and so can contribute towards defining its significance'.[50]

Interpretation of the universal laws (but not as a general rule, the particular i.e. local law) of the Latin Rite Church is delegated to the Pontifical Council for the Interpretation of Legislative Texts. It is not a tribunal. Its decisions are not appealable. It cannot fix laws that are wrong or outdated nor can it invent laws, though it does have some latitude to broaden or narrow the

---

48.   John P. Beal, James A. Coriden, and Thomas J. Green, eds, *New Commentary on the Code of Canon Law* (Mahwah NJ: Paulist Press, 2000) [Beal et al. in main text is Beal, Coriden and Green, *New Commentary* in footnotes], 73.

49.   Report of Commission of Investigation into Catholic Archdiocese of Dublin, Dublin, 2009, 78.

50.   See Herwi Rikhof, 'Vatican II and the Collegiality of Bishops; a Reading of *Lumen Gentium* 22 and 23' in *Collegiality Put to the Test*, eds James Provost and Knut Walf, *Concilium* (London: SCM Press, 1990), 4.

application of an extant law.[51] This body, which has no Civil Law equivalent, offers interpretations of particular ecclesiastical laws on an *ad hoc* basis usually in response to a request for clarification or to address a perceived error or confusion arising from implementation of the law. Its views are authoritative but on the subject of collegiality it has been silent.

Interpretations of the law by the Legislator (or delegated authority) sometimes take the form of laws themselves. In other cases interpretations may be informal, non-legally binding comments by the Legislator (a mode quite often used by the Pope), which while lacking legal status as 'authentic interpretations' nonetheless 'have doctrinal value'.[52]

An essential pathway to understanding any particular law, whether canonical or civil, lies in the specific, sometimes specialist, meaning ascribed to the key terms used in the construction of the law. In Civil Law, there are generally two primary sources of such meanings: the first, where legislation is concerned, is the definition of terms contained within the legislation itself. It is not unusual for Civil Law statutes or statutory instruments to have a section entirely devoted to definitions of terms. As a result of a deliberate decision of the Code Commission no such systematic definition of recurring or key terms exists in *CIC* or its predecessor *CIC/17*, though one will find occasional key terms defined *en route* through the Codes.

Even allowing that *CIC* treats of complex and often metaphysical subjects not easily amenable to definition, it is worth remarking that collegiality is not one such subject. The difficulties experienced at the Council and since have less to do with defining collegiality *per se* and more to do with disagreement about two fundamental issues, the first regarding the church's divine constitution and the second to do with ecclesiastical politics. The issue of the church's divine constitution arises in the context of the question, how is the College of Bishops to exercise its (divinely ordained) supreme and full power outside of Ecumenical Councils? The issue of ecclesiastical politics (also seen as a constitutional issue by some writers) is about the

---

51.   See Beal, Coriden and Green, eds, *New Commentary*, 72.
52.   Ibid., 71.

extent of active involvement of general members of the church in its governance. 'Collegiality' has, rightly or wrongly, become the shorthand for both these debates, its meaning stretched or narrowed to suit the perspective of the commentator.

The second primary source of meaning at Civil Law is found in reported and published case law where judges explore and expound meaning. Interpretations from higher appellate courts will carry at least considerable weight and may even be binding. The church has only a limited system of canonical courts dealing largely though not exclusively with marriage law. It has a quasi-appellate structure with its own ersatz precedent/praxis, a dearth of published authoritative case law, and certainly none that defines 'collegiality'.

Apart from *CIC* and *CIC/17* which will be discussed later, the other main searchable primary sources of juridic meaning are sacred scripture, tradition and certain documents, mainly authored by the Pope and the Ecumenical Councils. Some of these documents are valuable in discussing collegiality; pre-eminent among them is one of the foremost documents of Vatican II, the Dogmatic Constitution of the Church, *Lumen gentium*. There is an abundance of published documents from the Pope, the Ecumenical Councils, Synods, Pontifical Councils and Commissions, episcopal conferences, diocesan and parish bodies, many of which offer insights into the meaning of collegiality but which are of variable legal status in terms of their authoritative nature. They may be highly influential or even persuasive but many of them cannot be regarded as primary sources from a juridical point of view. For example, is the *Nota* to *LG* which is discussed below a primary or secondary source? *LG*, as a conciliar document is obviously a primary source. The *Nota* was not voted on by the Council Fathers but added as an appendix by the Theological Commission to the Council, with the approval of Pope Paul VI. While logic dictates the *Nota* be discussed alongside *LG*, it should be noted that its legal status is disputed.

1.7 Scripture

Scripture does not mention collegiality or colleges but certain relationships within scripture have characteristics consistent with general descriptions of collegiality. The twelve apostles are an

identifiable and stable group, each called to a clear and even exclusive membership. They were selected from a larger and looser
group of disciples to a kind of inner circle. There was an election
to fill a vacancy among 'the twelve'. They had a defined leader
in the person of Jesus Christ to whom they gave allegiance and
they in turn were looked to by the larger group of disciples as
leaders. They sublimated their individual wants and needs to
the greater good of the group and in furtherance of its shared
vision and purpose. Throughout the gospels they constitute a
definable and ring-fenced grouping. Whether they constitute a
juridical 'college' and whether if they do, what that might mean
juridically, is even two thousand years later a subject of debate.

Much scholarly discussion in the church about scripture and
collegiality has been about the bishops and the Pope as succes-
sors to the apostles and Peter respectively. It has largely foc-
ussed on governance and authority and how these roles are distributed between the College of Bishops and the Pope. Apart
from the mix of views within the Roman Catholic Church, this is
also, as mentioned above, an area of difference between the
Roman Catholic and other Christian Churches. The latters' concern is not so much with the primatial nature of the papacy
(though papal infallibility is a stumbling block for some) but
more to do with the extent to which the College of Bishops is
excluded from participation in day to day universal church governance. This is a major obstacle to Christian unity according to
Archbishop John R. Quinn:

> Large segments of the Catholic Church as well as many
> Orthodox and other Christians do not believe that collegiality
> and subsidiarity are being practiced in the Catholic Church in a
> sufficiently meaningful way. The seriousness of our obligation
> to seek Christian unity sincerely means that this obstacle to
> unity cannot be overlooked or dismissed as if it were the quirk
> of malcontents or the scheme of those who want to undermine
> the papacy.[53]

In its 1998 report The Anglican-Roman Catholic International
Commission points to 'collegiality, conciliarity, and the role of

---

53.   John R. Quinn, 'The Claims of Primacy and the Costly Call to Unity',
       Commonweal, 12 July 1996.

laity in decision making' as areas where 'though there has been convergence … a necessary consensus has not yet been achieved'.[54] While the report acknowledges convergence on the 'need for a universal primacy exercised by the Bishop of Rome as a sign and safeguard of unity within a re-united church' it reasserts 'the need for the universal primate to exercise his ministry in collegial association with the other bishops'.[55] More recently the Ecumenical Patriarch Bartholomew I speaking at the XII Ordinary General Assembly of the Synod of Bishops of the Catholic Church, remarked that the Orthodox Church

> … attaches to the Synodical system fundamental ecclesiological importance. Together with primacy synodality constitutes the backbone of the church's government and organization … this interdependence between synodality and primacy runs through all the levels of the church's life: local, regional and universal … our hopes are raised that the day will come when our two churches will fully converge on the role of primacy and synodality in the church's life, to which our common Theological Commission is devoting its study at the present time.[56]

Apart from noting these ecumenical difficulties, I do not propose to examine in depth the views of those other churches, though they have much of interest to say on the scriptural basis of collegiality and its meaning. The aspirations of Patriarch Bartholomew on synodality however, when aligned with comments by both Pope Paul VI and Pope John Paul II about the evolving nature of the Catholic Church's youthful Synod of Bishops, may yet hold an important key to future ecumenical convergence and to episcopal collegiality.[57]

---

54.   Anglo-Roman Catholic International Commission, 'The Gift of Authority' (1998): no. 3.
55.   Ibid., no. 1.
56.   Speech by Ecumenical Patriarch Bartholomew I to the XII Ordinary General Assembly of the Synod of Bishops, 26 October 2008, *Synodus Episcoporum Bulletin*, Holy See Press Office, English edition, www.vatican.va/news_services/press/sinodo/documents/bollettino_22_xii-ordinaria-2008/02_inglese/b30_02.html. [Accessed 05.4.2009].
57.   See Discourse of His Holiness John Paul II to the Council of the General Secretariat of the Synod of Bishops (30 April 1983) in *L'Osservatore Romano*, Weekly Edition in English, 23 May 1983, 5.

The Apostolic Constitution *Pastor bonus* supports the view that the collegial nature of the College of Bishops derives from scripture and from the Lord himself, though it makes an important observation about the bifurcated nature of the church's hierarchical constitution.

> The hierarchical constitution of the church … was endowed by the Lord himself with *a primatial and collegial nature at the same time* when he constituted the apostles 'in the form of a college or permanent assembly, at the Head of which he placed Peter, chosen from amongst them'. Here we are looking at that special concept whereby the pastors of the church share in the threefold task of Christ – to teach, to sanctify, and to govern: and just as the apostles acted with Peter, so do the bishops together with the bishop of Rome.[58]

Tierney cites scripture as evidence of an early tradition of collegiality that is close to Küng's collegiality of all the people of God. He says the early church 'was a community in which all participated in community life'. When the first major doctrinal issue arose it was settled by 'the apostles and elders with the whole church meeting in Council in Jerusalem (Acts 15:22)'.[59] Shortly after Vatican II, Cardinal Suenens, used two examples from scripture to support his (favourable) views on episcopal collegiality. The first was from Acts 2:14: 'Peter standing with the eleven, lifted up his voice and addressed them.' The second was from Acts 8:14: 'Now when the apostles at Jerusalem heard that Samaria had received the word of God, they sent to them Peter and John.'[60] By contrast Alfredo Cardinal Ottaviani, a Conciliar opponent of episcopal collegiality is reputed to have remarked during the Council that the only known reference to collegial action on the part of the apostles occurred as Christ was arrested in Gethsemane when according to Matthew 26:56 'they all fled'.[61] He declared that 'the collegiality of the apostles

58.   John Paul II, 'Apostolic Constitution *Pastor Bonus.*'
59.   See Brian Tierney, 'Church Law and Alternative Structures. A Medievalist Perspective' in *Governance, Accountability and the Future of the Catholic Church,* eds Francis Oakley and Bruce Russett (New York: Continuum, 2004), 61.
60.   See José De Broucker, *The Suenens Dossier: The Case for Collegiality,* 12.
61.   See John L. Allen Jr, *Cardinal Ratzinger: The Vatican's Enforcer of the Faith* (New York: Continuum, 2000), 46.

cannot be derived from the scriptures ... Anyone desiring to be a sheep of Christ must be shepherded by Peter and it is not for the sheep to lead Peter but for Peter to govern the sheep.'[62] Similarly the Bishop of Lerida is quoted as remarking that collegiality has no scriptural base.[63] Komonchak expresses the opposite view. '[I]n its full meaning based on scripture, episcopal collegiality, which succeeds to that of the twelve, is essentially universal.'[64]

1.8 Tradition

In LG we are reminded that

> ... the collegiate character and structure of the episcopal order is clearly shown by the very ancient discipline whereby the bishops installed throughout the whole world lived in communion with one another and with the Roman Pontiff in a bond of unity, charity and peace; it is also shown in the holding of councils in order to reach agreement on questions of major importance, a balanced decision being made possible thanks to the number of those giving counsel. Both of these factors are already an indication of the collegiate character and aspect of the episcopal order.[65]

Gallagher, points to considerable evidence of collegiality in the early church

> ... in the numerous synods of bishops that took place in the East and in the West throughout the first millennium. This was the exercise of joint responsibility of the bishops for the government of the church and it was done in every region in the early church.[66]

As for the canonical collections, Gallagher asserts that midway through the first millennium they show

> ... the normal way of going about solving problems, healing disunity or promoting Christian reform was to call a council of

---

62. See Alberigo and Komonchak, eds, *History of Vatican II: Mature Council*, 129.

63. Ibid., 126.

64. Joseph A. Komonchak, Introduction in *The Motherhood of the Church*, ed. Henri de Lubac (Ignatius Press, 1982), 18.

65. See Flannery, 29.

66. Clarence Gallagher, 'Collegiality in the East and the West in the First Millennium. A Study Based on the Canonical Collections', *The Jurist*, 64 (2004): 64.

the bishops of the region ... by mid-fifth century, synodical government was regarded as the norm ... Canon Law emerged as the sum of the decisions reached by bishops in council throughout the church.[67]

Tavard remarks on a Conciliar intervention by the Archbishop of Rouen to the effect that Pope Pius XII's Encyclical *Fidei Donum*[68] while it did not specifically use the term collegiality, nonetheless clearly affirmed the collegiality of the bishops.[69] He acknowledges however that there was no evidence of the collegial exercise of episcopal authority outside of Councils.[70]

Oakley accuses the church of conveniently forgetting its own conciliar history and consigning to 'institutional oblivion' a time when there was an 'age-old collegial and conciliar pattern of governance ... with potent memories of the ecclesiology of communion'.[71] The characteristics of that ancient collegiality (derived from the Roman law of sovereignty and of corporations) were that

> ... side by side with the institution of papal monarchy (and in intimate connection with it) it was necessary to give the church's communal and corporate dimension more prominent and regular institutional expression ... most notably by the assembly of general councils representing the entire community of the faithful and not necessarily limited in their voting membership ... to the ranks of the episcopate alone ... This conciliar and essentially constitutionalist pattern of thinking rose to prominence in the late fourteenth and early fifteenth centuries in the context of the Great Schism of the West.[72]

Tierney advances a similar argument:

> Within the Catholic tradition there have always been these three, Peter, the apostles, and the people of God but the constitutional relationships between them have been defined differently in

---

67.   Ibid., 65.
68.   Pius XII, Encyclical *Fidei Donum* (21 April 1957) in *AAS* 49 (1957), 225–50. English translation from Libreria Editrice Vaticana, www.papalencyclicals.net/Pius12/P12fidei.html.
69.   See George H. Tavard, 'Collegiality According to Vatican II', *The Jurist*, 64 (2004): 85.
70.   See ibid., 88.
71.   See Francis Oakley, *The Conciliarist Tradition: Constitutionalism in the Catholic Church, 1300–1870* (Oxford: Oxford University Press, 2003), 14.
72.   Ibid., 15.

different ages …. The modern practices of representation and
consent that characterise secular constitutional government are
not alien to the tradition of the church. And if in the future the
church should choose to adapt such practices to meet its own
needs in a changing world that would not be a revolutionary
departure but a recovery of a lost part of the church's own early
tradition. Within the sphere of ecclesiastical government the
task has always been to find a constitutional structure for the
church that reflects its own intrinsic collegial nature as a community of the faithful. The task was begun anew at Vatican
Council II. It is still far from completed.[73]

Tierney also argues that the governance structure of the church
has never been cast in stone but has taken many different shapes
over the centuries.

The church was not founded as a democracy … it was not
founded as an absolute dictatorship either. The first Popes did
not even claim the powers that modern ones take for granted.
They did not exercise jurisdiction over the whole church; it
did not occur to anyone that they were infallible; they did not
appoint bishops; they did not summon general councils.
Bishops were elected by their clergy and people and general
councils were summoned by emperors. It is a long way from
there to here. The church has been governed in different ways in
the past and it may be again in the future.[74]

Tanner claims that the church's long tradition of councils is
not only the world's oldest example of a representative assembly but predates by many centuries the Icelandic Althing of AD
930 which is often cited as the first instance of a parliamentary
assembly structure.[75] His views find an echo in Cotter's research
on general chapters of religious institutes. She draws attention
to 'a long tradition'[76] of collegial government by the general
chapter of religious institutes, which was given a fresh dynamic
by the conciliar doctrine of episcopal collegiality for it 'suggested
a different approach to the issue of governance at all levels of the

---

73.   See Brian Tierney, 'Church Law and Alternative Structures. A
       Medievalist Perspective', 60–1.

74.   Ibid., 50.

75.   See Norman Tanner, *Was the Church Too Democratic? Councils, Collegiality
       and the Church's Future* (Bangalore: Dharmaram Publications, 2003), 6.

76.   See Elizabeth M. Cotter, *General Chapter*, 70.

church'.[77] 'One of the by-products of renewal for religious was the reclaiming of those democratic structures that were enshrined in tradition: the collegial way of making decisions with the involvement of as many of the membership as possible.'[78] A clear link is made between tradition and collegiality and between collegiality and democracy. A further important link is made between the conciliar views on episcopal collegiality and how the spirit of those views was extracted, translated, and applied to other realms. The absorption of this derived collegiality into governance structures of religious institutes was relatively rapid and spontaneous, underlining Cotter's argument that it was essentially a return to old roots which had been interrupted by a period of rigid hierarchicalism, rather than an embrace of something entirely radical and new. 'Under the impetus of an on-going renewal, the church in Vatican II has, we believe, begun the journey towards redefining its authority as service in terms of the original vision of Jesus Christ.'[79]

Ivereigh echoes that view:

> Collegial governance is counterposed to the autocratic, centralist model which reached its apex in the mid-19th century. It is, in many ways, the more traditional model, one that prevailed in the first centuries of the church and which was represented by the 'conciliarists' of the Middle Ages.[80]

1.9 Codex Iuris Canonici 1917

Until the 1917 Pio-Benedictine Code (*CIC/17*), the Canon Law of the Catholic Church was uncodified. It consisted of the accreted laws of almost two millennia, some long since out of use though never officially repealed. The body of laws was vast and it was not held in any systematic way but comprised a clutter of both official and private partial collections as well as a large amount of supplementary laws, all or any of which might need to be

---

77.   Ibid.
78.   Ibid., 188.
79.   Ibid., 322.
80.   See Austin Ivereigh, 'Through the Vatican White Smoke', *Open Democracy*, 4 April 2005 in www.opendemocracy.net/faith-catholicchurch/article_2402.jsp. [Accessed 12. 10. 2008.]

interrogated to find the answer to a canonical query.[81] Roman
law often supplied the default position in the event that a particular matter was not covered by Canon Law. Pope Benedict XV
in promulgating *CIC/17* spoke of how the church had 'reformed
and brought to Christian perfection the very law of the Romans,
that wonderful monument of ancient reason'.[82]

The frustrations engendered by such an archaic, dilatory and
unwieldy system were evident in the early preparations for
Vatican I when a number of bishops mooted the need for simpli-
fication and codification. Pope Pius X took up the monumental
task in 1904. From the outset it was universal and collaborative,
seeking the opinion of every bishop. Representatives from every
nation participated in the College of Consultors which had the
task of overseeing the distilling of advice, gathering and pruning the plethora of laws and drafting the canons of the Code.
The project was not designed to change the extant law but rather
to make it more accessible. Twelve years later, on its completion
under Benedict XV, it could have been easily described as a
truly collegial labour though no such word appeared in
connection with its introduction. The Apostolic Constitution,
Providentissima Mater Ecclesia which promulgated *CIC/17*, did
have the following to say which is of considerable interest in the
context of the debate on the role of the College of Bishops at
Vatican Council II: 'Pius … considered it necessary to consult
the bishops whom the Holy Ghost had placed to rule the church
of God, so as to know fully their mind on this matter.'[83] Years
later, Pope John Paul II would use very similar language in promulgating *CIC* inviting the question whether both Codes were
more of a collegial than personal exercise of papal authority.

It was not long before *CIC/17*'s unfitness for a frenetically
changing contemporary world was exposed. For all of its applicable lifetime, from 1917 to 1983, the working language of *CIC/17*
was Latin. Translations into other languages were prohibited to

---

81.   See Peters, ed., *CIC/17*, 8.
82.   Benedict XV, 'Apostolic Constitution *Providentissima Mater Ecclesia*', 27
      May 1917 in *AAS*, IX (1917) pars II. 7. English translation in Peters, ed.,
      CIC/17, 21–4.
83.   Ibid.

protect the textual unity and integrity but this greatly inhibited access by the faithful including priests, bishops and even canon lawyers.[84] In fact Peters', the first available full text English translation, was published twenty years after *CIC/17* had been replaced by *CIC*.

CIC/17 continued in effect until the advent of *CIC* but as Peters reminds us the old law 'has not been wholly discarded'.[85] Although *CIC* (c. 6 §1) explicitly abrogates the old Code it also provides that where the new law reproduces the old the former is to be read in the light of 'canonical tradition' (c. 6 §2) and in case of doubt the revocation of the old law is not to be presumed but rather the old and the new should be related to one another and harmonised as far as possible (c. 21).

If *CIC* can be accused of using words like 'college' and 'collegial' in a variety of ill-defined circumstances then the same complaint can be made of *CIC/17*. Many canons in that Code pertain to 'colleges' without specifying what a 'college' is. 'Collegial' is used to differentiate certain entities from things associated with a cathedral or to indicate a 'collegial act', or to indicate a gathering of more than one.

Beal et al. assert that long before the Second Vatican Council or the drafting of the new Code, the concept of a 'college' had been 'juridically loaded down by Roman law and burdened by certain interpretations during the history of the church'.[86] These interpretations included an insistence on equality among the members and plenary convocations of all the members in order to make decisions. Within the canons of *CIC/17* there is micro-scopic attention to details governing elections and other set-pieces involving standard protocols. This preoccupation with due process, and checks and balances which are designed to ensure that individual members get the chance to input their voice is replicated in *CIC*. They would do justice to any organisation secular or ecclesial, attempting to create egalitarian, if quite bur - eaucratic, structures of inclusive governance. One can see that if

---

84. See Report of the Commission of Investigation into the Catholic Arch-diocese of Dublin, Dublin 2009, ch. 4.

85. See Peters, ed. *CIC/17*, xxv.

86. See Beal, Coriden and Green, eds, *New Commentary*, 430.

they were routinely applied to the College of Bishops outside of an Ecumenical Council, that is to say if the College were acknowledged as such a juridic college in the context of its authority to govern, it would radically reconfigure the current governance structure of the church. *CIC/17* however, mentions neither the College of Bishops nor its 'supreme and full power over the universal church' (*LG* 22). Instead *CIC/17* (c. 228) provided (aside from primatial power) that 'An Ecumenical Council enjoys supreme power over the universal church.'[87]

CIC/17 attributes many descriptions and titles to the Pope but Head of the College of Bishops is not one of them. That title, though of long history in the church,[88] is reserved to *CIC* (c. 331) and Beal et al. suggest that this 'emphasises the primacy of the Pope more so than did the corresponding provisions of the earlier code'.[89]

The codification process that gave rise to *CIC/17* was a colossal project, culminating in an document accessible at least to Latin scholars, which was a reservoir of centuries of church law but as Peters remarks, 'though long in gestation, its working shelf-life was in church terms comparatively brief, a mere sixty-five years'.[90] As Hervada-Lombardía says 'the basic problem with *CIC/17* was not so much its age but its conservatism.'[91] Effectively *CIC/17* was fossilised before the ink was dry on its codification. This, as we will see later, presented problems to those drafting *CIC* who were mandated to give legislative effect to the decisions of Vatican II, provide for its *novus habitus mentis* and still reconcile it with the juridic tradition summarised in *CIC/17*.

1.10 Other Sources of Meaning

Church approved texts can offer assistance, some as primary and others as secondary sources of meaning. *The Catechism of the Catholic Church* published by the United States Conference of

---

87.   See Peters, ed., *CIC/17*, 96.
88.   Beal, Coriden and Green, eds, *New Commentary*, 432.
89.   Ibid., 424.
90.   See Peters, ed., *CIC/17*, 10.
91.   *Exegetical Commentary*: vol. 1, 115.

Catholic Bishops contains a glossary written by then Archbishop now Cardinal William Levada and former Prefect of the Congregation for the Doctrine of the Faith. While the Catechism received papal approval, the glossary was an add-on to certain editions only and as such was not part of the approval process. In the glossary 'collegiality' is defined as the principle that

> ... all the bishops of the church with the Pope at their Head form a single 'college,' which succeeds in every generation the 'college' of the twelve apostles, with Peter at their Head, which Christ instituted as the foundation for the church. This college of bishops together with, but never without, the Pope has supreme and full authority over the universal church.[92]

This definition, while it fails to clarify the practical relationship between collegial and primatial power, does appear to locate papal primacy within the College of Bishops, a position much disputed between theologians.

Many scholarly analysts and learned commentators have written on the subject of collegiality. The views of eminent canonists are accorded considerable deference but not all analysts are canonists. Some are theologians, historians, pastors or ecclesially literate journalists. Ivereigh,[93] who could be said to belong to the theologically literate journalist sphere, describes 'collegiality' as '... the closest word that Catholics have to democracy. It does not refer to the question of sovereignty, suffrages and franchises: the legitimacy of the Pope and the bishops derives from the assurance of the Holy Spirit transmitted through the offices handed down by the apostles, and not from any kind of general will. But collegiality is a model of church governance which stresses the importance of collaboration between the Pope and his bishops, and respect for the local church as the primary locus of decision making'.[94]

---

92. See *Catechism of the Catholic Church: Modifications from the Editio Typica*, 2nd edition (Washington DC: United States Catholic Conference, 1997), www.usccb.org/catechism/text/glossary.html. [Accessed 01.9.2008.] NB The glossary is not part of the approved text.

93. Former Head of Public Affairs for Cardinal Cormac Murphy O'Connor, Archbishop of Westminster, and written while in post.

94. Ivereigh, 'Through the Vatican White Smoke.'

Örsy describes 'collegiality' in similarly broad and juridically vague terms:

> It is a seminal term, not well defined but pointing far and wide. We keep progressing in its understanding – rich concepts yield their content slowly. For this reason, I cannot give you a final definition but I can offer a fair explanation – enough to work with. 'Collegiality' is a term used mainly in the western church; it means to operate in a collective manner, as distinct from a strictly and exclusively monarchical government. Let examples speak: whenever an ecumenical council is in session, namely, when all the bishops are deliberating and deciding as a 'corporation' with the Pope presiding, they are acting collegially. Similarly, when the bishops of a territory gather in conferences, or when the priests of a diocese assemble around their bishop, or when the faithful participate in a pastoral synod, they are working collegially, although in various ways and to different degrees. (The idea of collegiality does not exclude an internal hierarchical structure: the bishop of Rome has the role of the Head in the bishops' college with a power that the members do not have. His eminent power, however, needs to be integrated organically with the power of the others without being subordinated to them.) ... Such collegial actions, in truth, are the external expressions of an internal unity that we call 'communion'. This internal and invisible unity is created by God's own actions.[95]

Both Örsy and Ivereigh cast the net of collegiality wide but wrap it in communion. Others, like Quinn are reluctant to describe as collegiality, collaboration on agendas over which one has no control.[96] Writing of his work for Pope John Paul II in relation to religious life, he says that the Pope

> ... thinks in collaborative terms and ... his personal style is marked by openness to ask for help and a willingness to listen. Yet these are instances not so much of collegiality as they are of collaboration by bishops in a task undertaken by the Pope at his initiative ... collaboration by bishops with the Pope in a task he specifically entrusts to them is not the full measure of collegiality ... Collegiality does not exist in its fullest sense if bishops are merely passive recipients of papal directives and initiatives. Bishops are not only *sub Petro*. They are also *cum Petro*.[97]

95. See Örsy, 'Peter and Paul Seminar: The Unfinished Work of Collegiality.'
96. Former President of the American Episcopal Conference and Pontifical Delegate for Religious Life in the United States.
97. See Quinn, 'The Claims of Primacy and the Costly Call to Unity.'

Quinn claims that Pope John Paul II 'specifically mentions collegiality'[98] in the encyclical *Ut unum sint* in the following quotation, though the word collegiality is not used:

> When the Catholic Church affirms that the office of the Bishop of Rome corresponds to the will of Christ, she does not separate this office from the mission entrusted to the whole body of bishops, who are also 'vicars and ambassadors of Christ'. The Bishop of Rome is a member of the 'college' and the bishops are his brothers in the ministry.[99]

This description, like Levada's, arguably sees primatialism within the context of collegialism rather than independent of it but it also does not explain how it is that in practice the Pope appears to operate juridically in two spheres, one a free-ranging primatial sphere and the other the sphere of the College of Bishops of which he is Head, a body to which he never reports though it is a standing body. The constitutional/theological implication of this question is profound. It is beyond the scope of this book and so far has eluded theological consensus. Whether or not the Pope has two distinctive streams of authority (and his conciliar recognition as Head of College of Bishops was designed to head off any lurking constitutional difficulties) the question still arises as to whether irregular Ecumenical Councils are an adequate exercise of the powers of governance of the College of Bishops.

Arrieta, in his discussion on 'colleges' and 'collegiality', says that in Canon Law

> … the juridical concept of 'college' refers to a type of collaboration between members in the decision making process, as well as a unity in acting upon the decision made … It does not necessarily imply equality among members of the college. The principle of collegiality represents above all, a way of defining the collective will of the organ (or a way of reaching this objective), as well as 'assuming' the decision made. Collegiality is a system of participation for arriving at decisions through dialogue of all the members in a discussion … the final decision is not referred

---

98.   Ibid.
99.   See John Paul II, encyclical *Ut Unum Sint*. 25 May 1995 in *AAS*, 87 (1995), 921–82. English translation from Libreria Editrice Vaticana, www.vatican.va /edocs/ENG0221/_INDEX.HTML. [Accessed 01.9.2009.]

to as an agreement – but rather deliberations … this system obviously assumes that individuals are open to dialogue, detached
from personal opinions and desire the harmonisation of personal opinions. In addition the principle of collegiality imposes on
the members of the college a duty to assume the final decision as
their own … and a duty to execute the decision reached.'[100]

This juridical definition of a 'college' is at odds with the so-
called 'strictly' juridical meaning attached to the same word by
the *Nota* in which equality among college members is said to be
presumed. It is in line with the general norms provisions in both
CIC/17 and *CIC* where it is evident that collegial structures are
generally expected to involve participation by members in
decision making. Equality among members is not presumed and
hierarchical structures are not ruled out but provision is required for decision making through which the collective will is
expressed and put into effect. Though Arrieta mentions 'dialogue of all the members' the question of delegated or representative participation remains open as does the mode of participation which while most easily met by plenary or even virtual
convocation could also be met by any alternate mode which
facilitates dialogue among the full membership. Arietta's view
does not however match the provision for conciliar collegiality.

Walf points out that while the word 'college' is a juridical
notion, its juridical character is not what was intended by *LG*
nor was it what was translated into *CIC*'s provision for conciliar
collegiality especially in cc. 330–41. This was 'apparently to be
restricted to a non-juridical, purely pastoral meaning'.[101] So we
have the irony that juridically *CIC* gives effect to a non-juridical,
pastoral collegiality while at the same time repeating and updating (particularly in the section on General Norms) long established juridic practice regarding colleges and collegial proced -
ures. Herranz is correct that the words 'collegiality' and 'colleg -
ial' are frequently used with little juridical precision'[102] and the
use of the same terms in the same document for different things

---

100.   See Juan Ignacio Arrieta, *Governance Structures within the Catholic Church*,
       Gratianus Series (Montreal: Wilson and Lafleur, 2000), 74.
101.   See Beal, Coriden and Green, eds, *New Commentary*, 423.
102.   See *Exegetical Commentary*, vol. 1, 144.

was a recipe for confusion. The more basic problem however was fundamental disagreement about church governance at the First and Second Vatican Councils. The latter hosted the main debate on collegiality and church governance so it is to Vatican II that I now turn for the views that came to guide *CIC* and conciliar collegiality.

CHAPTER TWO

The Second Vatican Council and Collegiality

2.1 Introduction: Unfinished Business of Vatican I

Vatican II's contentious discussion of collegiality owed much to Vatican I which had broken off before its discussions were complete, as the Franco-Prussian War broke out. It never resumed, but collegiality did feature even in the truncated discussions. There was opposition to an episcopal collegiality which involved a juridic college of equals. It was feared that collegiality was dangerously difficult to pin down and could prove inimical to unity and to primacy. The preference for rule by one strong, all-powerful voice was deliberate in the context of the unstable, global political canvas of the day and the ambient secular political structure which was dominated by monocracies.

Papalism won out over conciliarism with clear declarations on papal primacy and papal infallibility but no clarity on the governance role or juridic status of bishops. These questions were left hanging until the next Council but in the long interim the church was shaped by Vatican I. Institutional attitudes and practices developed around a monocratic papacy in which bishops were seen as delegates of the Pope. Meanwhile the world changed and by the time Vatican II opened its doors in a new post-colonial, post-monocratic, democratising era, the unfinished agenda of Vatican I was clamouring to be dealt with. The decision of Pope John XXIII to convene a new Ecumenical Council rather than simply reconvene the interrupted Vatican I, indicated the level of disconnection from that past which even a church immersed in tradition could not ignore.

2.2.1 Vatican II

Collegiality became the most discussed and divisive subject at Vatican II. *LG* distilled that fractious debate into a less than lucid consensus which was then further compromised when the *Nota* was appended to the *Constitution*. It quickly became a subject of great controversy both within and outside the Council. To understand some of the pressures and perspectives which were in play during those heady days, it is necessary to look at the Council's views on collegiality in their broader setting within the world and within *LG* itself.

2.2.2 *Within the World: The Broader Setting*

A backward glance to the world of Pope John XXIII is important. The Pope often said his mission was to cultivate a garden, not to guard a mausoleum, echoing the words of St Paul 'You are God's field',[1] and foreshadowing the words of *LG* (5), 'The church is a cultivated field, the tillage of God.' If there were elements of the mausoleum about the church as Pope John XXIII found it in 1959, it is hardly surprising. If there was a palpable pressure towards updating that too is hardly surprising though the metaphor of cultivating a garden suggests something more akin to careful, planned pruning, weeding and planting rather than anything revolutionary or convulsive. Europe in particular had been through quite a lot of the latter.

The landscape of twentieth century-Europe had been radically altered by industrial scale war, the evil of the Holocaust in which historic Christian anti-semitism had played an ignoble part[2], the fall of many dictatorships and autocracies, the advance of egalitarian democratisation and modern secular states, the liberation of women, widened access to education, the militancy of atheistic communism and the shifting axis of power as the masses flexed their political, intellectual and economic muscle as never before. These followed through in uneven but evident progression from the liberal, modernising ideologies set in train from the time of the French Revolution.

A decade before the Pope's convocation of the Council, a remarkable event had taken place, with the promulgation of the Universal Declaration of Human Rights.[3] For the first time in

---

1.   1 Corinthians 3:9.
2.   See 'Building on Nostra Aetate. 50 years of Christian–Jewish Dialogue.' 5th Berrie Lecture given by Cardinal Koch, President Pontifical Council for Promoting Christian Unity and Commission for religious relations with Jews. Pontifical University of St Thomas Aquinas, Rome, 16 May 2012.
3.   See United Nations General Assembly, 'Universal Declaration of Human Rights', 1948.

human history the governments of the world had unanimously agreed a set of inherent and inalienable rights common to all people, everywhere and for all time. Those rights applied to every individual human being as their birthright, regardless of race, religion, ethnicity, gender, disability, age and sexual orientation. Though of moral rather than legal status, a significant consequence of the Declaration was that the great walls of state (and church) became penetrable and permeable; their treatment of citizens (members) was opened to observation, measurement and accountability to the entire human family against the benchmark of the Declaration. It gave rise to or helped to encourage what Nobel Laureate Seamus Heaney has called 'a grammar of imperatives, the new age of demands'.[4]

The twentieth century had become a very uncomfortable place for privileged ruling elites who dribbled out begrudged concessions to their subjects. The new grammar included the right of people to have their say in the things that concerned them, the right to equality of citizenship and the right to structures which were capable of vindicating their rights. In traumatised post-war Europe, fresh thinking would lead to a radical shift away from conflict and competition between nations towards the most remarkable adventure in collegiality ever undertaken in democratic politics, the European Union.

The Treaty of Rome, the founding treaty of the Union, was a mere two years old when Pope John XXIII announced the Council. The post-war period with all its contradictions, liberation for some, sectarian, Soviet or communist oppression for others, was a time of widespread catharsis as the flame of civil rights consciousness prised open exclusive and elitist authority structures, letting in a different future. A newfound freedom, determined and headstrong was putting confidence into the once silent or voiceless or the simply overlooked and another burgeoning phenomenon, the mass media, still in its infancy, was for many, their ally and their conduit to a wide audience. The world of science and technology already shifted out of its low grade agricultural kilter by the first industrial revolution was advancing rapidly towards the second. Human brainpower

---

4.   Seamus Heaney, *New Selected Poems 1966–1987* (London: Faber and Faber, 1990), 236–7.

rather than brawn was the engine of the second industrial revolution and education was its fuel.

Seamus Heaney put it more poetically:

> And next thing, suddenly, this change of mood.
> Books open in the newly wired kitchens.
> Young heads that might have dozed a life away
> Against the flanks of milking cows were busy
> Paving and penciling their first causeways
> Across the prescribed texts.[5]

The centuries old, hierarchically structured institution that is the Roman Catholic Church found itself part of an altered and altering world. Pope John XXIII knew that the church too would have to change, for already its members were part of the foment of the time. The church could not simply hope to stand unmoving and intact while this tsunami of change washed over it. The Pope's decision to convene Vatican II was part of a much more generalised pattern of major shifts that were occurring in the wider world and that with hindsight we can see as a watershed in human history. In many societies men and women were struggling to redefine and reshape secular authority and governance structures. The key, challenging words were 'equality' and 'inclusion'. Örsy's comment on the dangers of immovable laws in evolving societies seems particularly apt: 'either the laws will break the community or the community will break the laws.'[6]

In Montgomery, Alabama in 1955, Rosa Parks refused to give up her seat on a bus to a white person as required by the laws of racial segregation. The American Civil Rights Movement was born. A striking painting by Audrey Flack of an early Civil Rights march is entitled 'Sisters of the Immaculate Heart Marching.' It shows a number of white nuns right at the front of the march for civil liberties for African Americans.[7] The 'sixties' was to be the era of widespread civil rights agitation and for

---

5.   Ibid.
6.   See Ladislas M. Örsy, *Theology and Canon Law: New Horizons for Legislation and Interpretation* (Collegeville, Minn: Liturgical Press, 1992), 63–4.
7.   See Fiona Kearney, ed., *Modern American Paintings from the NYU Art Collection* (Cork: Glucksman, 2004), 95.

more than a few those struggles were only successful after pro-
longed agitation including in some cases, periods of awful vio-
lence. Within the church, among the laity and clergy that same
unrest and fresh creativity that characterised the secular world,
was also at work, indeed many church members were active
contributors to the debates in both spheres and on all sides,
liberal and conservative alike.

The bishops of the world brought to the Council their own
direct experience of these still raw and relatively undistilled
changes. Some had been champions of change, others had not.
Some welcomed the emerging world. Others dreaded it. They
came from dictatorships with which they were on good terms,
dictatorships which they opposed, democracies where the
church flourished and democracies where it was under pressure, from the poorest countries and the richest and all points in
between. No two were the same. The scene was set for lively discussions, though somewhat disappointingly given the breadth
and depth of rights-based debate going on in the secular world,
the liveliest debate in the Council was on a subject in which each
bishop had a personal interest, the subject of episcopal collegiality, in other words the issue that most touched on their own status, rights and responsibilities. In that respect they were completely in touch with the times for it was an era replete with
special interest groups which were pleading their own causes.

Even before the Conciliar debate, the signs of dissension on
church governance were already evident in the preparatory
Schema on the church which

> ... did not try to harmonise the powers of the Pope and the pow-
> ers of the College; it defined them by juxtaposition and related
> them to each other on the basis of the fact that in exercising its
> authority the college had to take account of the supremacy of its
> Head. The lack of a canonical way of regulating the two powers
> compelled the *Schema* to recall at this point 'the non-canonical
> nature of the hierarchic structure' in order to explain the balance
> between the two.[8]

The tentativeness of *Schema* in this regard would ultimately
dog the deliberations and the decisions of the Council itself. It

---

8.   Alberigo and Komonchak, eds, *History of Vatican II: Mature Council*, 65.

was not only expressive of deeply held and opposing views within the episcopacy but it touched on a neuralgic subject which had been festering for a century and which was being re-visited in a rather giddy world context. A few decades later such tentativeness might have been less evident; indeed their preoc-cupations might have been considerably broader than the im-mediate self-interest of the debate on episcopal collegiality.

Tagle has argued that Paul VI's contributions to the conciliar debate on episcopal collegiality are key to understanding the outcome and its complexity.

> Vatican II was episcopal collegiality in action. The role of Paul VI in the development of the Vatican II discussions, in the reso-lution of the controversies that arose, in the conclusion of the council, and later on in the implementation of the council's orientations and directives, instructs us on how the Petrine ministry keeps episcopal and ecclesial communion intact in an increasingly pluralist episcopate and church. Reading how Paul VI kept 'the boat afloat' during both the turbulent moments of the council and the difficult period that followed it, makes us thank God for the gift of the papal ministry as the centre of stability, unity and direction for the pastors of the church and for the entire ecclesial community.[9]

The conciliar struggle between primatialists and collegialists, according to Ratzinger, resulted in a 'consequent ambiguity ... a sign that complete harmony of views was neither achieved nor even possible'.[10] This is in some ways a classic example of the very essence of collegial consensus, for one of the strengths of collegial processes is their capacity to hold the integrity of the group together even in the face of internal dissension. However, to safeguard that very unity, the failsafe valve of an acceptable level of ambiguity is sometimes used and clarity falls victim to it as the decision tries to be all things to all people. In such circum-stances the gravitational pull of conservatism can be irresistible. To some extent this is what happened to collegiality in *LG*. That it did, should not be such a surprise when one looks at the state

---

9.   Luis Antonio G. Tagle, *Episcopal Collegiality and Vatican II: The Influence of Paul VI*, Landas Monographs (Manila, Philippines: Loyola School of Theology, 2004), Preface.

10.   Ratzinger, *Theological Highlights of Vatican II*, 115.

of flux in the wider world of the conciliar era where many of the radical forces which were mustering were meeting resistance and where it would be years before they began to bear fruit in the projects like the end of apartheid in the United States and Africa, equal rights for Catholics in Northern Ireland, equal opportunities for women, gay rights, the death throes of imperialism and colonialism, the levelling of the Berlin Wall, the break-up of the Soviet Union and the end of communist domination of the Baltics and Eastern Europe. Many of these projects and a lot more besides are still works in progress. Among them can be counted conciliar collegiality.

A universal church headed by a Pope (even one as benign as John XXIII) whose power of governance had all the hallmarks of autocracy and which had not been significantly updated since 1870, was always going to encounter difficulties in adjusting to the mounting of new realities both within and without. This was especially so when among those realities was pressure for greater inclusivity and accountability in institutions unaccustomed to either concept and lacking in self-updating mechanisms that could have provided a graduated pathway to change. The Council tried to make *LG* a major part of the blueprint for that new pathway. *LG*'s internal architecture and content were destined to carry the weight of future centuries.

2.2.3 *Within* Lumen Gentium: *The Broader Setting*

The Council fathers were asked by the Council commission to answer a number of questions concerning the status, role and powers of bishops. The answers showed overwhelming support for the view that the bishops were not delegates of the Pope and that by divine authority, the College of Bishops (with its Head and never without its Head) had full and supreme authority over the universal church. These responses formed an import - ant part of the seminal conciliar changes reflected in *LG*. They effectively opened the still continuing debate on how that collective episcopal authority over the universal church is to be exercised.

At the request of the Council fathers, *LG* reversed a crucial and long-standing order of importance when it placed the chapter on the People of God (*LG* ch. 2) before the chapter on the hierarchy (*LG* ch. 3) and acknowledged the common priesthood of all the faithful. This represented a fundamental radical re-ordering of the relationships within the church which until then had been presented as a series of receding tiers, with the laity at the bottom, the priesthood above the laity, the bishops above the priests and the Pope above everyone. It was a top-down model of governance with everyone below the top offering simple and unquestioning obedience to the Pope. Channels of communication flowed downwards only. Upward feedback was not encouraged. *LG* flattened the pyramid, at least in theory. The church was redrawn as a communion of all the baptised faithful, 'the new People of God' (*LG* 9) whose Head is Christ. As for the relationships between the faithful there was to be

> … no inequality on the basis of race or nationality, social condition or sex … And if by the will of Christ some are made teachers, pastors and dispensers of mysteries on behalf of others, yet all share a true equality with regard to the dignity and to the activity common to all the faithful for the building up of the Body of Christ (*LG* 13).

The twentieth century language of aspirational inclusivity was well in evidence. The tone and content matched the contemporary secular mood but the test would come later when the lofty sentiments were translated into actuality and benchmarked experientially against the high-minded language.

In the guiding principles of the Code commission, the notion of equality of all the faithful set out so emphatically in *LG*, was to be the foundation stone on which would rest all juridic rights and responsibilities set out in the new Code. Governance and authority were to be seen as 'service' rather than 'rule'. The People of God were seen as being co-responsible for the church's mission though each had different roles.

LG's recognition of the supreme and full power of the College of Bishops broke new ground. Under *CIC/17* there was no mention of such an entity much less its supreme power. Now the College of Bishops (with its Head and only with its Head) was acknowledged as a locus of divinely ordained supreme power but how was that power to be exercised? The answer unfortunately was not spelt out in *LG*. Just as Vatican I had broken off at a critical juncture leaving unfinished business, Vatican II ended inconclusively leaving in place no mechanism (except the Pope) for working out the practical implications of episcopal collegiality, though some had hopes that Paul VI's institution of the Synod of Bishops would fill the gap and advance the debate. The conciliar road map to collegiality was little more than rudimentary. Ironically the failure to be specific about the implications of collegiality while giving it such notoriety facilitated the growth within a variety of universal and particular church sectors of a rising tide of expectation, ambition, impatience and creativity around governance and inclusivity. Given the mood of the historic moment in which the Council took place, many groups within the church were looking for words and concepts to latch onto which would assist their calls for greater inclusivity. Collegiality, with its 'one-size fits all' stretchability, was ready made for their purposes.

This background forms a necessary platform from which to approach an understanding of the notion of shared responsibility or co-responsibility as well as effective and affective collegiality within *LG*, *CIC* and their subsequent development in different areas of Church life. It had profound consequences for the Council's exploration of the relationship between the Pope and the bishops, both as individuals and as a college. It shaped the development of the Synod of Bishops and episcopal conferences. It informed the subsequent debates on governance in many institutes of religious life and gave rise to a range of different outcomes.[11] It was an important component of subsequent inter-church ecumenical dialogue. It also encouraged the gradual and still modest growth of formal and informal inclusivity, at other levels in the church, particularly of the laity. These have been mostly in decision making rather than decision taking processes, with mixed results, so far.

2.3 Lumen Gentium *and collegiality*

Nowhere in *LG* is the People of God, described as a 'college' nor is the word 'collegial' used to describe its internal relationships. Where the words, 'college', 'collegial' and 'collegiate' occur in *LG* they are used virtually exclusively in the context of either the

---

11.   See Elizabeth M. Cotter, *General Chapter*, ch. 3.

apostolic college comprising Peter and the other apostles, or
the College of Bishops comprising all the bishops throughout
the world including the Pope, in language which Komonchak
describes as a 'non-technical' and 'elastic'.[12] There is however
one exception which says that this collegial unity

> ... is apparent also in the mutual relations of the individual bish-
> ops with the particular churches and with the universal church
> ... the episcopal bodies[13] of today are in a position to render a
> manifold and fruitful assistance, so that this collegiate feeling
> may be put into practical application (*LG* 23).

Sobanski argues that this is a clear acknowledgment that collegiality

> ... is not just limited to acts of the episcopal college – in the sense
> of its totality along with its Head. So collegiality as a property of
> the office of bishop is seen by the council both in the vertical and
> horizontal dimension. This leaves the way open to seeing colle-
> giality in the broader ecclesial context. This direction is taken
> both by the statements of the magisterium and in the literature
> after the council.[14]

Sobanski features among the commentators mentioned
above who believe that conciliar collegiality was intended to be
sans frontières, not restricted to Episcopal College governance of
the universal church but encountered and developed at national,
regional and diocesan level. He also describes how in consequence of *LG*, an expectation was created of greater momentum
towards a spirit of collegiality in the wider church structures,
bearing in mind however that *LG* was ever careful to assert
the hierarchical structure of the church and in particular that
the Pope's 'power of primacy over all, both pastors and
faithful, remains whole and intact' (*LG* 22). This collegiality ap-
proximates to a pervasive spirit of cooperation but Komonchak
contradicts the accuracy of such a use, saying of episcopal

---

12.   See Joseph A. Komonchak, 'The Significance of Vatican Council II for
      Ecclesiology' in Patrick Granfield and Peter C. Phan, *The Gift of the Church:
      A Textbook Ecclesiology in Honor of Patrick Granfield OSB* (Collegeville,
      Minn: Liturgical Press, 2000), 87.
13.   Note that in some translations this is given as 'conferences'.
14.   See James H. Provost and Knut Walf, *Collegiality Put to the Test*, Concilium
      (London: SCM Press; Trinity Press International, 1990), 45–53.

conferences in particular that the Council 'did not say that in their conferences the bishops carry out their responsibility "collegially" but they carry it out "conjointly". Their immediate purpose is practical and local and therefore cannot be considered collegial'.[15] This highlights a conviction shared with some commentators that collegiality is exclusively associated with the exercise of episcopal power at universal church level. Episcopal conferences by this reckoning would be excluded from the juridic description of collegial. As we will see in the Council's Declaration on the Pastoral Role of the Bishops *Christus Dominus* (*CD*),[16] the section on Episcopal Conferences does not mention collegiality and the limited mention of collegial/collegiate action is confined to episcopal collegiality in the sense of universal governance, not local or regional. *ApS*[17] confronts this debate head on, insisting that the College of Bishops acting in its entirety is the only forum to which the juridic term 'effective collegiality' can apply. Everything else is affective collegiality at best; it lacks the strong juridic significance of the College of Bishops and is generally no more than structured cooperation. It is not clear how this reconciles with *LG*'s assertion that collegiate unity exists in the mutual relations of individual bishops to particular dioceses and to the universal church (*LG* 23) though significantly this care and solicitude of individual bishops for the whole church is not 'exercised by any act of jurisdiction' (*LG* 17).

While *LG* acknowledges the centrality of the People of God and states that all the faithful share in 'the one priesthood of Christ' (*LG* 10) the words associated with 'collegiality' fade from the text of *LG* once it has finished talking about the episcopacy. By the time it moves on to priests, deacons, religious and the laity such words are entirely absent.

The laity are said to share, in their own way, in the three *munera* (*LG* 31) but their role in relation to the *munus* of governance is generally intended to be one of passive obedience; 'the

15. See Joseph A. Komonchak, Introduction in Thomas J. Reese, ed. *Episcopal Conferences: Historical, Canonical and Theological Studies*, 18.

16. See Vatican II, Decree Concerning the Pastoral Office of Bishops in the Church; *Christus Dominus* (28 October 1965) in *AAS*, 58 (1966) 673–96, English translation in Flannery, 283–315.

17. See John Paul II, Apostolic Letter *Apostolos Suos* (21 May 1998).

laity should accept in Christian obedience what is decided by
the pastors who as teachers and rulers of the church, represent
Christ' (*LG* 37). They can, though, be called 'in different ways to
more immediate cooperation in the apostolate of the hierarchy
… they may … be appointed to certain ecclesiastical offices
which have a spiritual aim' (*LG* 33). The word 'cooperation' as
used here indicates certain limits; the laity has no entitlement to
such a role and it is for the hierarchy to decide the nature and extent of any such cooperation. These provisions however represented a unique and historic opportunity for somewhat extended
inclusion of the laity. They created a groundswell of expectation
and ambition from which came the more generalised and ad-
justable use of the words, collaboration, co-responsibility and
collegiality to describe a greater post-conciliar lay involvement
in church affairs. Used in such contexts, collegiality at best describes a mood or spirit rather than a juridic entitlement and at
worst it is a poor fit as became evident in 1997 when the Vatican
moved to inhibit lay 'collaboration' in the sacred ministry of the
priest for fear that lay collaboration was going too far.[18]

Strangely the words 'college' and 'collegiality' are absent
from discussions on religious life. Above all aspects of church
life, the religious institutes have the clearest collegiate nature
and have become the most advanced area of the church in terms
of developing the practical internal architecture of collegial
structures. *LG* takes pains to emphasise the over-arching hierarchical right to regulate, supervise and approve the conduct of religious life. Even allowing for that, however, many religious institutes have, in the light of Vatican II, engaged in processes of
deep introspective discernment out of which have evolved considerably more collegial structures and processes.[19] It is hardly
coincidental that such institutes have standing, active, governance fora which were able to facilitate sustained debate and
change.

---

18. See Congregation for the Clergy, Instruction on Certain Questions
    Regarding the Collaboration of the Non-Ordained Faithful in the Ministry
    of Priests *Ecclesiae de Mysterio* (15 August 1997): *AAS*, 89 (1997), 852–77.
    English translation from Libreria Editrice Vaticana, www.vatican.va
    /roman_curia/pontifical_councils/laity/documents/rc_con_interdic_d
    oc_15081997_en.html. [Accessed 01.9.08.]
19. See Elizabeth M. Cotter, *General Chapter*, ch. 3.

In its acknowledgment of the church as the People of God and its reordering of hierarchicalism as service to the People of God, *LG* moved the language of the church (whatever about the church itself) into a new era. These concepts were to be like leavens at work throughout the universal church and at every level, shifting the rigid top-heavy structure of the pre-conciliar era. By far the biggest issue of juridic significance tackled by the Council fathers was the role of the College of Bishops in relation to the governance of the universal church and it is that same role which absorbs much of *LG*'s discussion of collegiality.

LG grounds the episcopal collegiality of the College of Bishops in Christ's actions when he constituted the apostles 'in the form of a college or permanent assembly over which he placed Peter chosen from among them,' (*LG* 19) though of course the Lord Jesus Christ remains the supreme high priest. Interestingly in translations of *LG* other than Flannery's, the more diluted words 'stable group' appear instead of the sharper-edged 'permanent assembly'.

The discomfort with the notion of a 'college' of bishops and in particular its juridical implications, is evident at various points in the document where efforts are made to indicate the merely approximate rather than exact nature of the terminology. For example there is reference to 'the college or body of bishops' (*LG* 22). What is clarified, ending decades of controversy, is that the bishops are not mere delegates of the Pope charged only with powers of governance over their particular churches. Instead they serve individually by divine authority and collect - ively they constitute the College of Bishops which has, also by divine authority, 'supreme and full power over the universal church' (*LG* 22). The College of Bishops is always united with its Head, the Pope, and its decisions require his consent (*LG* 22).

The college's authority can be exercised in Ecumenical Councils which can only be convened by the Pope and are subject to his authority regarding both the content of the agenda and decisions. *LG* acknowledged that the College of Bishops could act outside of Councils when the bishops are dispersed throughout the world, provided it acted in unity with the Pope who either calls them to collegiate action, 'or at least approves of or freely accepts the united action of the scattered bishops, so that it is thereby made a collegiate act' (*LG* 22). To date it has never happened but some commentators believe the College of Bishops could initiate such action (indeed there are distant historical precedents) without advance approval by the Pope though it requires that he 'at least approves ... or freely accepts' the action before it can be 'a truly collegiate act' (*LG* 22).

Theoretically then the College of Bishops could function governmentally (with its Head) outside of an Ecumenical Council if an effective means could be found to gather the views and votes of several thousand men scattered across globe or if a valid system of representational delegation could be put in place (though some Council fathers thought delegation impossible, a view shared it seems by Pope John Paul II and articulated in *ApS*[20]). The *Schema* on the church had already 'courageously provided for the possibility of hitherto unknown ways of exercising the powers of the college.'[21] Despite advances in communications technologies Caparros et al. are sceptical about the likelihood of more regular involvement of the College of Bishops in governance.

> When considering the past and looking into the future, it does not seem likely that collegiality in its strictest sense will be practiced more assiduously from now on. Indeed 'the college' although it is always in existence is not for that reason continually engaged in strictly collegiate activity. In other words it is not always in full activity; in fact it is only occasionally that it engages in strictly collegial activity.[22]

Not every decision requires the mammoth effort expended in preparing for Ecumenical Councils or drafting the two Codes which were undertaken before the advent of the internet, email, teleconferencing etc. Technology has now made a global opinion trawling process and teleconferencing somewhat more practicable and holds out possibilities for greater access, speed and regularity, particularly if problems of wireless availability, encryption and security of transmission of data can be credibly

20.   John Paul II, Apostolic Letter *Apostolos Suos*.
21.   See Alberigo and Komonchak, eds, *History of Vatican II: Mature Council*, 66.
22.   See Ernest Caparros, Jean Thorn, and Michel Thériault, *Code of Canon Law Annotated: Prepared under the Responsibility of the Instituto Martín De Azpilcueta*, 2nd ed. (Montréal: Wilson & Lafleur, 2004), 279.

overcome. As these technologies develop, new options for exercising the authority of the College of Bishops may in time come
into view. *LG* certainly did not close off such possibilities but
neither did it set up the structures necessary to transform the
College of Bishops into an active standing governmental forum.
Instead *CIC* provides that the Pope can select ways in which the
College of Bishops may function collegially (c. 337 §3).

Under *LG* the Pope's power of primacy remains 'whole and
intact' (*LG* 22). He too has full, supreme and universal power of
governance over the whole church which he can exercise personally or collegially at his discretion and without being an-
swerable to anyone or any forum. No attempt is made to reconcile this with the power of the College of Bishops but the Pope
though Head of the college has no required reporting relationship to it. *LG* says there can be no college without its Head;
whether there can be a Head without his college is still grist to
many theological mills. No answer is provided to the theological question whether the Pope's divinely instituted personal
and collegial authority represent two independent strands of
authority or one unified strand exercised as Head of the College
of Bishops.

In practical terms the church's day to day governance by
the Pope assisted by the Curia remained untouched by Vatican
II. Outside of Ecumenical Councils the College of Bishops is
regarded as exercising episcopal collegiality by its passive
maintenance of communion and solidarity, a position also un-
changed since Vatican II.

Oakley asserts that

> ... as a result of these manifestly uneasy formulation ... the
> church would now appear to possess not one but two agencies
> endowed with supreme ecclesiastical authority; the supreme
> pontiff acting alone and the college of bishops united with
> its papal Head,'[23] and there exists no 'inbuilt governmental
> mechanism capable of imposing practical constitutional restraints
> on the freewheeling exercise of that primatial authority.[24]

---

23.   See Francis Oakley, *The Conciliarist Tradition: Constitutionalism in the
       Catholic Church, 1300–1870*, 11.
24.   Ibid., 13.

2.4 The Preliminary Explanatory Note: Nota Explicativa Praevia
Although tensions between primatialism and conciliarism/col-
legialism were evident throughout the conciliar debate on
collegiality, at all times there was consensus on the Pope's primacy, Headship of the College of Bishops and his overarching
power of veto. Even so the primatialists remained to be con-
vinced, seeing in even the most circumscribed version of collegiality a threat to the Pope's authority which they worried would
come to be seen as existing only by virtue of being Head of the
College rather than by virtue of his succession to Peter. The
Council's Theological Commission, with the approval of the
Pope, attached an Explanatory Preliminary Note (*Nota*) to *LG*,
which according to Ratzinger 'injected something of bitterness
into the closing days of the session'.[25]

The *Nota* was never voted on by the Council. It appears in an
appendix to *LG* and its exact juridical status as mentioned earlier
is still disputed. Ratzinger says the *Nota*

> ... did not create any substantially new situation. Essentially it
> involved the same dialectic and the same ambiguity about the
> real powers of the college as the Council itself manifested.
> Without doubt the scales were here further tipped in favour of
> papal primacy as opposed to collegiality. But for every state-
> ment advanced in one direction the text offers one supporting
> the other side and this restores the balance, leaving interpreta-
> tions open in both directions. We can see the text as either 'pri-
> matialist' or collegial. Thus we can speak of certain ambivalence
> in the text of the 'explanatory note', reflecting the ambivalent
> attitude of those who worked on the text and tried to reconcile
> the conflicting tendencies.[26]

LG and the *Nota* left episcopal collegiality in a definitional
limbo but the *Nota* offered what it claimed was a strict juridical
meaning of the word 'college'. The formula derived from classic
Roman law, says 'College in a strictly juridical sense is 'a group
of equals who entrust their power to their president' (*LG Nota* 1).
Quinn says adoption of this inflexible view of collegiality was
unnecessary and something of a cynical exercise on the part of
the Council fathers who were opposed to episcopal collegiality.

---

25.   See Ratzinger, *Theological Highlights of Vatican II*, 115.
26.   Ibid.

Clearly a College of Bishops of equals, would threaten Petrine Primacy.[27] The *Nota* says firmly that the College of Bishops is not to be regarded as a college in this strict juridical (Roman) sense.

The *Nota* claims that in church jurisprudence a 'college' has a fixed meaning which demands equal membership. However where the word 'college' is used in *LG*, and it is extensively used there, it means something else entirely, though quite what is not made clear. In particular the College of Bishops 'is not understood in a strictly juridical sense, that is, as a group of equals who entrust their power to their president, but as a stable group whose structure and authority must be learned from Revelation' (*LG Nota* 1).

Örsy says of the *Nota* that through a

> … somewhat informal intervention by Paul VI, an uneasy truce and compromise was imposed on the two contending parties. The minority received an assurance that the statements on collegiality in *LG* must not be interpreted in a way that would harm the traditional doctrine of primacy. The majority was reassured that the already approved texts of the constitution firmly upholding collegiality would not be touched.[28]

He also cautions that asking what the Council fathers meant exactly by collegiality is

> … an ill conceived enquiry because the fathers never spoke with great precision; in fact they never agreed on a definition. They left behind an open affirmation They did what other councils did: they intuited a mystery, stated its existence and left it to future generations to explore its depth and breadth.[29]

Inevitably there were conflicting views about the impact and intent of the *Nota*. Some described its introduction as a 'black week', a setback for ecumenism and a dilution of the view of the majority at the Council.[30] It is hard to challenge Ratzinger's

---

27. See John R. Quinn, *The Reform of the Papacy: The Costly Call to Christian Unity. Ut Unum Sint: Studies on Papal Primacy* (New York: The Crossroad Publishing Company, 1999), 84.
28. See Ladislas M. Örsy, 'A "Notion" of Collegiality', *The Jurist*, 64 (2004): 36.
29. Ibid., 37.
30. See Guissepe Alberigo and Joseph A. Komonchak, eds, *History of Vatican II*, vol. IV (New York: Orbis, 2004), 460–4.

conclusion that the failure to achieve harmony on the issue at the Council resulted in a deliberate post-conciliar ambiguity about the powers of the College of Bishops. This ambiguity was to be subsequently imported into the Code of Canon Law and its clarification remains as significant a challenge for the church of the 21st century as it did for the church of the 19th and 20th centuries.

2.5 Other Vatican II Documents

Although *LG* dominates any review of conciliar collegiality, it was only one of sixteen seminal conciliar documents, each individual yet inter-related and all collectively forming the legacy of Vatican II. Common themes and repetition run through the documents but while the word 'college' crops up occasionally the principle of collegiality does not. Remarkably the Pastoral Constitution on the Church in the Modern World *Gaudium et spes*[31] makes no mention whatever of 'collegiality' but the Dogmatic Constitution on the Sacred Liturgy *Sacrosanctum concilium*[32] *(SC)* uses the word 'college' in the context of liturgical celebrations presided over by 'the bishop surrounded by his college of priests and by his ministers' *(SC* 45). The word 'college' is used without definition or further explanation which begs the question whether it is to be 'strictly' juridically interpreted and if it is what does that mean in practical terms for the 'college of priests'? Karl Rahner asked if it 'was not proper to say something about the collegiality of the presbyteral order? For presbyters are not only individual collaborators of the bishop, they constitute, as it were, the bishop's senate'.[33] Two years later came the promulgation of the Vatican II Decree on the Ministry and Life of Priests *Presbyterorum ordinis*[34] *(PO)* where the words

---

31.   See Vatican II, Pastoral Constitution on the Church in the Modern World *Gaudium et Spes* (7 December 1965) in *AAS*, 58 (1966), 1025–124, English translation in Flannery, 163–282.

32.   See Constitution on the Sacred Liturgy *Sacrosanctum Concilium* (4 December 1963) in *AAS*, 56 (1964), 97–134, English translation in Flannery, 117–61.

33.   See Guissepe Alberigo and Joseph A. Komonchak, eds, *History of Vatican II: The Formation of the Council's Identity: First Period and Intersession October 1962–September 1963*, vol. II (New York: Orbis, 1997), 314.

34.   See Vatican II, Decree on the Ministry and Life of Priests *Presbyterorum Ordinis* (7 December 1965) in *AAS*, 58 (1966), 991–1024, English translation in Flannery, 317–64.

'college' and 'collegiality' made no appearance at all. Instead the word 'collaboration' was used to describe the role of priests in relation to their bishops.

> Priests are made in the likeness of Christ the Priest by the Sacrament of Orders, so that they may, in collaboration with their bishops, work for the building up and care of the church which is the whole Body of Christ, acting as ministers of him who is the Head (PO 12).

By contrast the decree on the Missionary Activity of the Church *Ad Gentes*[35] (*AG*) promulgated on exactly the same day as *PO*, refers to the 'college of priests' (*AG* 19), the 'college of apostles' (*AG* 38), the 'College of Bishops' (*AG* 38) and to a 'collegial spirit' (*AG* 6). It does not define or describe the characteristics of these concepts nor does it deal with their juridic significance. It says that 'The bishops, in turn, each one together with his own college of priests, being more and more imbued with the mind of Christ and of the church, feel and live along with the universal church' (*AG* 19). This sheds little light on any juridical implications for the college of priests, though the following extract does have something more to say on that subject.

> The local priests in the young churches should zealously address themselves to the work of spreading the gospel, and join forces with the foreign missionaries who form with them one college of priests, united under the authority of the bishop (*AG* 20).

There are structural and juridic implications here in the assertion that both local and missionary priests form one college and that they are united under the authority of the bishop. The role of the bishops in evangelising is described in interesting terms given the acknowledgment in *LG* of their supreme and full power.

> All bishops, as members of the body of bishops succeeding to the College of Apostles, are consecrated not just for some one diocese, but for the salvation of the entire world. The mandate of Christ to preach the gospel to every creature (Mark 16:15) primarily and immediately concerns them, with Peter and under Peter. Whence there arises that communion and cooperation of

---

35.   See Decree on the Church's Missionary Activity *Ad Gentes Divinitus* in *AAS*, 58 (1966), 947–90, English translation in Flannery, 443–97.

churches which is so necessary today for carrying on the work
of evangelisation (AG 38).

It is difficult to know whether the reference to Christ's
preaching mandate as being the bishops' primary and immediate concern is in any way deliberately loaded to subliminally
contextualise their universal teaching role as being of more immediate concern than their universal church governance role.
The bishops are not even collectively referred to as the College
of Bishops yet we are told that their 'missionary activity… exercises the collegial spirit of her hierarchy' (AG 6). AG offers no
further clarity on collegiality; few if any of the Council decrees
do.

The Decrees Optatam totius,[36] on priestly training, and
Perfectae caritas,[37] on religious life, are silent where one might
have expected some reference at least to the spirit of collegiality.
Similarly Orientalum Ecclesiarum[38] which deals with the Eastern
Rite churches, makes no mention of it, nor does Inter mirifica[39]
the decree on Social Communications. The Decree on the Laity,
Apostolicam actuositatem[40] references 'colleges' in the educational
sense of a school, another variety of 'college' recognised juridically but yet not conforming to the idea of a strictly juridical college in the terms set out in the Nota. Those references add nothing much to our understanding of the idea of juridic collegiality
within the church though as we will see later the decree's views
on the laity, add something to our understanding of co-responsibility and possibly affective collegiality. Besides AG, the only
other significant references occur in Christus Dominus (CD), on
the pastoral role of the bishops and Unitatis redintegratio[41] (UR),
the decree on ecumenism.

---

36.   See Decree on the Training of Priests Optatam Totius (28 October 1965) in
       AAS, 58 (1966), 713–17.
37.   See Decree on the up-to-date Renewal of Religious Life Perfectae Caritas
       (28 October 1965) in AAS, 57 (1964), 5–75.
38.   See Decree on the Catholic Eastern Churches Orientalium Ecclesiarum (21
       November 1965) in AAS, 57 (1965), 76–9.
39.   See Decree on the Mass Media Inter Mirifica (4 December 1963) in AAS, 56
       (1964), 145–57.
40.   See Decree on the Apostolate of Lay People Apostolicam Actuositatem (18
       November 1965) in AAS, 58 (1966), 837–64.
41.   See Decree on Ecumenism Unitatis Redintegratio (21 November 1964) in
       AAS, 57 (1965), 76–89.

Since *CD* deals with the pastoral role of bishops it is no surprise to find significant back referencing to *LG*. The bishops 'As
far as their teaching authority and pastoral government are concerned ... are united in a college or body with respect to the universal church of God' (*CD* 3). Neither the term 'college' nor
'body' is defined and the relationship between the college and
its Head is set out in extracts taken directly from *LG*, so that no
gap can be opened up between the two documents.

Fresh issues do arise, however, from *CD*. The first, is the assertion that the Synod of Bishops will

> ... render more effective assistance to the supreme pastor of the
> church in a deliberative body which ... since it shall be acting in
> the name of the entire episcopate ... will ... show that all the
> bishops in hierarchical communion partake of the solicitude for
> the universal church (*CD* 5).

The description of the Synod as a deliberative body acting in the
name of the entire episcopate (which equals the College of
Bishops so why not use that term?) is of profound importance
because that is not how the Synod has turned out. *CD* does not
mention collegiality nor any juridic relationship between the
Synod of Bishops and the powers of governance of the College
of Bishops. Is it a body with delegated authority from the
College of Bishops or from the Pope? Are its deliberations made
in the name of the college? If it is as *CD* says acting in the name
of and 'representative of the entire Catholic episcopate' (*CD* 5)
why does it only have a reporting relationship to the Pope and
not to the body it is said to represent? I will return to these questions later when looking in more detail at the Synod of Bishops.

The second interesting issue in *CD* is that the words 'college'
and 'collegiate'/'collegial' appear only in the section which
deals with the relationship of bishops to the universal church.
Unlike *LG* no such phraseology is used in dealing with the part -
icular church, or Episcopal Conferences though there is talk of
'collaboration' (*CD* 16), 'cooperation' (*CD* 17) and 'harmonious
activity' between bishops and priests (*CD* 21) and between bishops and those involved in pastoral activity at particular church
level (*CD* 29). Thus *CD* reinforces the line which limits collegiality proper to the universal governance role of the College of
Bishops.

As mentioned earlier, collegiality is contentious in ecumenical dialogue. In a decree designed to enhance ecumenical dialogue there was a thorny path to be navigated and so we find in
UR an unsurprising litany of words and phrases designed to encourage 'fraternal dialogue', 'friendly collaboration', 'concord'
and 'cooperation'. 'Collegiality' is absent. Conciliar opponents
of collegiality saw it as opening floodgates that could lead to the
kind of disunity they associated with the collegial governance
structures of the Reformation Christian churches. Recent difficult debates within the Anglican Communion would not, in
those quarters, be seen as making collegiality attractive. The collegiality at work in those churches was perceived as a recipe for
doubt. The reverse was also argued by those who saw collegial
governance as a more authentic validation of both centralised
primatial power (the mandate of Peter) and the mandate Christ
gave to the apostles and through them to the College of Bishops.

UR uses only the word 'college'. It appears twice (UR 2 and
3) each time referring to the apostles as the 'College of Twelve'.
The apostles are described as a group and a college with Peter as
their Head. The three *munera*, teaching, ruling and sanctifying,
are unequivocally entrusted to the apostolic college which is
succeeded by the bishops, among whom is the Pope, who as
Peter's successor is their Head.

> Christ entrusted to the College of the Twelve the task of teach-
> ing, ruling and sanctifying … Jesus Christ, then, willed that
> the apostles and their successors – the bishops with Peter's
> successor at their Head – should preach the gospel faithfully,
> administer the sacraments, and rule the church in love (UR 2).

This unified model of church governance locates Petrine
power within the College of Bishops but in reality as already remarked elsewhere the Head of the college governs without direct input from the college as a college. The assistance given to
the Pope by individual bishops or Cardinals through the Curia,
the Synod of Bishops or College of Cardinals has no juridic link
to and is not formally representative of the College of Bishops.
The current system of universal church governance has been
described by David Willey (BBC's Vatican correspondent since
1972) as more comparable to a 'medieval court'.[42]

---

42.   See Willey, 'A Gaffe Too Far', 4.

Among the Council Declarations, *Dignitatis humanae*,[43] *Nostra aetate*[44] and *Gravissimum educationis*,[45] only the last uses the word 'college', but it does so exclusively in the context of educational establishments such as Catholic colleges and universities.

2.6 Conclusion

The Council documents, individually and collectively, illustrate the definitional fault-lines and frailties caused by the Council's unresolved ambiguities on collegiality and church governance and from the absence of a strong editorial hand which could have ensured a greater degree of consistency in the use of key terms especially those with distinct juridic character. As we will see from the wide variety of often unrelated and irreconcilable circumstance in which *CIC* uses the words 'college' and 'collegial' there is a stubborn failure of clarity and consistency that was also a feature of *LG* and that is not coincidental. They stand in stark contrast to the relative clarity of pre-Conciliar procedural and episcopal effective collegiality which the new Code also had to provide for. These problems were well known to the drafters of *CIC* and they could not have been unaware that they were setting the scene for ongoing difficulty in terms of interpretative intelligibility, given the public and seminal nature of *CIC*, its universal audience and the likelihood that these issues would not be revisited for a very, very long time.

---

43. See Vatican II, Declaration on Religious Liberty *Dignitatis Humanae*, 7 December 1963 in *AAS*, 58 (1966), 929–41.
44. See Declaration on the Relation of the Church to Non-Christian Religions *Nostra Aetate* (28 October 1965) in *AAS*, 58 (1966), 740–5.
45. See Declaration on Christian Education *Gravissimum Educationis*, 28 October 1965 in *AAS*, 58 (1965), 728–39.

CHAPTER THREE

The 1983 Code of Canon Law and Collegiality

3.1 Introduction: The Drafting and Revision Process

The 1983 Code of Canon Law was the culmination of a twenty-four year process of reform of Canon Law begun by Pope John XXIII. It was the vehicle through which the decisions of Vatican II were given legal effect.

> Although it was announced together with the ecumenical council, nevertheless it (the Code) follows chronologically because the work undertaken in its preparation, which had to be based upon the council, could not begin until after the latter's completion.[1]

The process began in 1959 when Pope John XXIII tasked a commission of bishops and cardinals (more than seventy participated), with writing a new Code. It was a colossal undertaking, not simply a tidying up exercise like *CIC/17*. The new Code was to express the *novus habitus mentis* of the Council. The commission started work in 1965, in the final days of Vatican II, setting up themed study groups of consultors. A draft set of guiding principles was presented to the 1967 Synod of Bishops for approval. Over the next five years or so the study groups drafted *Schema* which were circulated to every bishop, curial dicastery and academic faculty of Canon Law for comment. The bishops often held broader consultations within their own jurisdiction. The responses were distilled by the commission secretariat and the study groups. In 1980 an overall *Schema* was delivered to the Pope for scrutiny by the full membership of the commission. Their proposed amendments were then reviewed by the secret-ariat of the commission who issued a comprehensive report (the 1981 *Relatio*) setting out reasons for and against the commission's proposals. The *Relatio* came before a plenary meeting of the commission where it metamorphosed into the 1982 *Schema*.

---

1.   See *SDL*.

The Pope then considered the new *Schema* first in the company of an expert panel and later along with a small group of cardinals where it was once again subjected to changes. According to Burke, 'in order that the text be completely his own as the Supreme Pastor of the church, [the Pope] personally read the final draft of the 1983 Code, canon by canon, with the help of a select group of experts.'[2] Peters points out that there was 'considerable legislative activity during the eight months of papal review,'[3] evidence of not inconsiderable papal scrutiny and input. Only members of the commission voted on the near-to-final text but it was the Pope who 'closed' the document, gave it final approval and force of law.

Herrada-Levardía observes that 'the subject of the canonical sciences includes both divine law and human law.' This may explain why *CIC* can be a model of clarity one minute and consummate vagueness the next. Some matters concern theological rather than juridical science.[4] Yet Canon law has to accommodate both and so unsurprisingly given its theological and juridical complexities and conciliar ambiguities, 'the incorporation of the principle of collegiality proved to be the greatest difficulty in drafting the 1983 Code.'[5] Those who drafted *CIC* were not mandated to resolve the problems left unresolved by the Council and so inevitably those problems made their way into *CIC*.

Peters believes that a full understanding of the 'accomplishments and failings' of *CIC* depends on understanding the 'accomplishments and failings'[6] of *CIC/17*. *CIC* is not juridically umbilically separated from *CIC/17*. According to c. 23 of *CIC* we cannot presume that any former law has been replaced. Both old and new Codes remain in an ongoing relationship which confers continuing relevance on the old. Thus collegial structures and practices within *CIC/17* are of more than mere historic interest.

---

2.   See Foreword by Archbishop Raymond L. Burke in Edward N. Peters, *Incrementa in Progressu 1983 Codicis Iuris Canonici: With a Multilingual Introduction (English, Francais, Italiano, Espanol, Deutsch, Polski)*, Collection Gratianus is Gratianus Series. Research Tools (Montreal, Quebec: Wilson & Lafleur, 2005), VI.

3.   Ibid., XII.

4.   See *Exegetical Commentary*, vol. 1, 34.

5.   See Beal, Coriden and Green, eds, *New Commentary*, 425.

6.   See Peters, ed., *CIC/17*, xxv.

3.2 *The Apostolic Constitution* Sacrae Disciplinae Leges

The promulgation of the new Code was effected by Pope John Paul II through the Apostolic Constitution, *Sacrae disciplinae leges* (*SDL*). While not forming part of the Code this introductory document has the status of law.

Frederick McManus claims that in *SDL* Pope John Paul II 'added a new stress on key elements of the [conciliar] project'. These four key elements were, the church as the People of God and as communion, collegiality and primacy, participation of all the faithful in the three *munera* of Christ and commitment to ecumenism.[7]

References to the words 'collegial', 'collegially' or 'collegiality' appear seven times in *SDL* but with little attempt to explain their meaning. Some references describe the congenial working atmosphere created by all those involved in its drafting, where they exhibited an 'outstandingly collegial spirit'.[8] The word 'collegiality' is also used to describe more tellingly and technically, the very nature of the process itself. 'The note of collegiality eminently characterises … the process of developing the … code.'[9] *CIC* is described as the fruit of a 'collegial collaboration'[10] between specialists and institutions all around the world. Here 'collegial' describes the long and elaborate process of collabor-ation, debate, drafting and deliberation involving mainly in-house experts and the hierarchy.[11]

SDL emphasises that the Pope has the support of the bishops worldwide for the Code's introduction. This raises the question whether the promulgation was an exercise of personal or collegial papal power for the distinction between the two is often hazy. The strong view of Herranz, who worked on the drafting of *CIC*,[12] and of Coccopalmerio is that the Pope acted personally.[13]

---

7.   See Frederick R. McManus, 'Canonical Overview: 1983–1999' in Beal, Coriden and Green, eds, *New Commentary*, 9.
8.   *SDL*.
9.   Ibid.
10. Ibid.
11. The Preface to the Latin edition of the Code states that 'throughout the entire task there were 105 Cardinal Fathers, 77 archbishops and bishops, 73 secular presbyters, 47 religious presbyters, 3 religious, and 12 laypersons.'
12. See *Exegetical Commentary*, vol. 1, 132.
13. See Francesco Coccopalmerio, 'The Role of the Legislator in the Church' in *Annual Conference of the Canon Law Society of Great Britain and Ireland, May 5–9* (Rome 2008), 6–18.

John Paul II himself emphasises that while the technical promulgation of *CIC* is 'an expression of pontifical authority,' the content of the Code and the process of how its content was arrived at, was a widely inclusive process and distinctly collegial. More than that, in acknowledging (as Pope Benedict XV had done in relation to *CIC/17*) that his promulgation of *CIC* was in response to the wishes of the bishops 'of the whole world who have collaborated with me in a collegial spirit'[14] the Pope was noting the fundamental importance of obtaining collegial consensus through active collaboration. This alludes to the response by the global episcopacy to the invitation to collaborate in the preparation of the new Code. That invitation was itself, according to *SDL* an expression of *LG*'s vision of the church as the People of God and 'its hierarchical constitution based on the College of bishops united with its Head'. It is quite conceivable therefore that in promulgating the new Code the Pope was not simply exercising his authority personally but in a very real sense, collegially as Head of the College of Bishops. This view may not be compatible with Coccopalmerio who stated as an 'undisputed premise that the author of the Code of Canon Law (both Latin and Eastern) is the Pope, the successor of Peter, who holds the office of Primate and is therefore the legislator for the universal church'.[15] Insofar as the Pope must authorise and promulgate all universal church law it is appropriate to describe him as 'the legislator', but to describe him also as 'the author' is at best a term of exaggerated deference given the many authors (including the Pope) of *CIC*.

It was always envisaged according to *SDL* that the long process of drafting *CIC* would allow for 'as collegial a method as possible'.[16] Here 'collegial' refers to the range of roles played by the bishops over the course of the Code's preparatory years. A tiny number were intimately involved on a regular or full-time basis through the secretariat or the commission or the study groups. Others, by far the vast majority, made submissions either as individuals or through their respective episcopal conferences. The entire College of Bishops was consulted. In this

14.   See *SDL*.
15.   See Francesco Coccopalmerio, 'The Role of the Legislator in the Church', 7.
16.   *SDL*. .

dispersed consultation and centralised process of distillation, Pope John Paul II saw a form of ersatz conciliarism for he asserts that *CIC* 'by analogy with the council ... should be considered the fruit of a collegial collaboration because of the united efforts on the part of specialised persons and institutions throughout the whole church'.[17]

If *SDL* has interesting things to tell us about collegiality and the process which created *CIC*, it also has important things to say about collegiality and the substance of the laws contained in the Code. The 'outstandingly collegial spirit' which as we saw above was applied to the drafting process is also said to apply 'to the very substance of the laws enacted'.[18] There are a number of possible interpretations of this reference. Is it simply saying that the arrival at agreement on the substance of the laws was subject to a collegial process leading to consensus or is it suggesting that the laws themselves incorporated the conciliar call for greater collegiality in new structures, practices and procedures? If it means the former then it is no more than an unnecessary repetition of what has already been said about the laborious drafting process. The weight of subsequent remarks in *SDL* favours the second suggestion.

> This note of collegiality, which eminently characterizes and distinguishes the process of origin of the present Code, corresponds perfectly with the teaching and the character of the Second Vatican Council. Therefore the Code, not only because of its content but also because of its very origin, manifests the spirit of this Council.[19]

Thus *CIC* originated from an exercise of collegiality; collegiality forms part of the teaching and character of the Council and *CIC*'s content expresses conciliar collegiality. An intriguing aspect of *SDL*'s views on collegiality is visible in its discussion of 'the mark of newness in the Code'.

> Among the elements which characterise the true and genuine image of the church, we should emphasise especially the following: the doctrine in which the church is presented as the People of God (cf. *LG*, no. 2), and authority as a service (cf. ibid., no. 3);

---

17.   Ibid.
18.   Ibid.
19.   Ibid.

the doctrine in which the church is seen as a 'communion,' and which, therefore, determines the relations which should exist between the particular churches and the universal church, and between collegiality and the primacy.[20]

Here the doctrine of the people of God and hierarchical authority as service, are both clearly and specifically back-referenced to *LG*.[21] There is no such back reference for the doctrine of the church as communion or for collegiality. Nor is collegiality specifically limited to the context of episcopal collegiality. Although it is mentioned over and against its relationship with the primacy, it is placed firmly within the context of the entire church as a communion and authority as service, not rule.

3.3 Collegiality Generally in the 1983 Code of Canon Law

The word 'collegiality' is not used at all in *CIC*, a curious omission of a word which played so dominant a role in the course of Vatican II and which was used so liberally in the introduction to *CIC*. Cynics might see in this the glossy packaging of less than glamorous contents to make them appear more attractive than they are in reality.

The shift from the language of theology to Canon Law does not fully explain such an omission for *CIC* is a legal document like no other. It accommodates many words and concepts which are difficult to comprehensively define, including that other great Vatican II doctrine of the church as 'communion' which gets somewhat better attention from *CIC*.

CIC was to be an important vehicle for translating the decis-ions of Vatican II into juridic form. The drafters had to take account of the Council's views, manage its ambiguities, provide for the development of the *novus habitus mentis* and maintain an umbilical link with past canonical tradition. These things weighed heavily on the drafters of *CIC* and according to Herranz[22] resulted in three distinct aspects of its treatment of collegiality.

---

20.   Ibid.
21.   *LG*, 2–3 in Flannery, 1–3.
22.   See *Exegetical Commentary*, vol. 1, 144.

Firstly, *CIC* covers a sphere of collegial activity which has strict juridic and largely procedural application (and is not conciliar collegiality at all). This is to be found mainly in the legal micromanagement of the internal structures of entities, such as certain lawfully established groups (some of which may be colleges of one sort or another). It covers concepts like collegial jur - idic persons and collegial acts and its purpose is to set out rules for the orderly and fair conduct of business of certain stable groups (including colleges) within the church. These rules mostly derive from *CIC/17*, albeit in updated form.

Secondly, the principle of conciliar collegiality was not applied 'to the common participation of all the faithful in the church's mission which is … the area of co-responsibility'.[23] This is particularly evident, as we shall see, in the tortuous process of getting agreement on the wording of *CIC* c. 129 which states that the laity can 'cooperate' in the exercise of the power of governance/jurisdiction. According to Herranz, *CIC* intentionally restricted the application of conciliar collegiality to governance at episcopal level. Below that level, he claims, the appropriate terminology is 'co-responsibility' (a term not used in either *LG* or *CIC*) but which includes 'cooperation' This distinction does not necessarily help to clarify what precisely 'collegiality' is but it does clarify what it is not.

Thirdly, *CIC* treated Conciliar collegiality, as applying to 'certain forms of carrying out the proper mission of the hierarchy'.[24] This collegiality is to be found in the College of Bishops and in joint action by groups of bishops such as particular councils. Whether it is at work for example in the Curia, the Synod of Bishops or *ad limina* visits or the growth of national, regional and supranational episcopal conferences will be examined below but it is by no means agreed that it is.

Bearing in mind these distinctions between procedural collegiality and conciliar collegiality, between co-responsibility and conciliar collegiality and between effective and affective collegiality, we can perhaps begin to analyse collegiality in *CIC*. As Miñambres points out the upshot is, that the fact that 'a

---

23.   Ibid.
24.   Ibid.

determined entity is called a college does not necessarily signify that in its actions it is governed by the principle of collegiality!'[25]

CIC is divided into seven books, each dealing with different aspects of the church's legal infrastructure. Words associated with collegiality are distributed throughout all seven books. Book Three is entitled 'The Teaching Office of the Church' while Book Four is entitled 'The Sanctifying Office of the Church.' There is no book dedicated to the third *munus*, governance, the one most associated with collegiality. Instead it is dealt with in Book Two entitled 'The People of God.' The order and manner in which subjects are dealt with are not arbitrary but follow the priorities set by the Council. The church as presented in *CIC/17* was a hierarchic monocracy. The church of *CIC* was to be 'The People of God.'

Although *CIC* is a collection of laws, its language strays from the dry technical to the richly theological, meandering from one register to the other, occasionally even in the same canon. Rather terse little procedural rules can sit close by grand and great visions for humanity. Canons move jerkily from the ontological, replete with divine mystery to the dully bureaucratic, from things collegial that have a clear juridic shape to things collegial which do not. This makes it impractical to simply scroll through the canons which concern collegiality in numerical order. Instead I group the canons thematically, dealing first with *CIC*'s technical/procedural provisions (procedural collegiality) which help unpack the idea of a 'college' and 'collegiality' albeit usually as pre-conciliar jurido/procedural concepts and then with *CIC*'s treatment of conciliar collegiality. The negligible read across between both is quite extraordinary as we will see.

3.4 Procedural Collegiality

All seven books of *CIC* have something to contribute to procedure and all use the words 'college', 'collegial', 'collegially' or 'collegiate' to a greater or lesser extent. The canons relevant to procedural collegiality come primarily from Book One with a smaller number from Books Two and Seven.

---

25.   See *Exegetical Commentary*, vol. I, 962.

Book One of *CIC* deals with General Norms and belongs to the technical domain. Many of the canons dealing with procedural collegiality have direct equivalents in *CIC/17* which have been updated and modified by *CIC* and so conceptually long pre-date Vatican II. Book One is rather like a book of instructions. It sets out the all-purpose, general rules which form 'the basic building blocks for the entire canonical system'.[26] These rules are of wide and general application. They establish the less glamorous inner workings of the canonical architecture of the church. The fact that the canons discussed in this section are procedural does not prevent them from having something important to tell about collegiality in church practice.

Book One[27] deals with 'juridic persons,' an artificial Canon Law entity not unlike a company or corporation in civil law. Such entities have legal rights, responsibilities and powers which mimic those of a physical person. In civil law, companies and corporations can only be brought into being by a legal process. Canon Law is similar. The status of juridic personality can only be conferred by a competent authority like the Pope, or a bishop. Once conferred, certain consequences follow in terms of the legal rules and regulations by which they must operate and the rights they must observe, in order for their conduct to be valid. The canons delineate the basic minima required for the organisational life of a juridical person to function satisfactorily and lawfully, bearing in mind the rights and obligations attaching to its members or possessions. In many cases *CIC*'s provisions can be overridden or enhanced by particular laws or norms and so often represent a default position.

Canon 115 explains the concept of a juridical person. There are two types, an aggregate of persons (*universitates personarum*) and an aggregate of things (*universitates rerum*). An aggregate of persons can be either collegial or non-collegial and an aggregate of things can be directed by a college. To be an aggregate of

---

26. See James Coriden, *An Introduction to Canon Law: Revised* (Mahwah, New Jersey: Paulist Press, 2004), 42.
27. The following canons of Book One use the words 'college', 'collegial', or 'collegiate'; cc. 115*, 119*, 120*, 127*, 140*, 158*, 160, 166*, 169*, 174*, 175, 176, 177, 182 and 183. C. 129* uses the term 'cooperate'. Only those asterisked are discussed below.

persons requires that there be three members at foundation stage and to be 'collegial' the members must 'determine its action through participation in rendering decisions whether by equal right or not' (c. 115 §2). If they do not so determine, then the juridic aggregate of persons is non-collegial. While c. 115 imitates the old Roman Law requirement of at least three people to found a 'college', a collegial juridic person is not necessarily a 'college' in the strict juridic sense encountered in the *Nota* to *LG* since equality among members is not essential. Given the *Nota*'s rigid view on the meaning of a 'college' it is perplexing that the first encounter with the words 'collegial' or 'college' in *CIC* should be in connection with a juridic entity which does not insist on equality among members and that the word 'college' should be undefined.

An example of a collegial entity is an Episcopal Conference or a religious institute. An example of a non-collegial juridic entity would be a parish for although it may embrace many parishioners, and even have consultative fora in which parishioners participate, they do not canonically determine parish action through participation in rendering decisions. That role juridically devolves to the pastor. Provision is made in *CIC* for parish and diocesan pastoral councils and finance councils with lay participation but they are advisory only, have no legal authority to act in the name of the parish and must in the case of finance councils 'be careful not to compromise the canonical function of the pastor as administrator of parochial goods'.[28]

In firmly identifying parishes and dioceses as non-collegial juridic persons, the Code commission rejected the case for making bodies like pastoral councils, diocesan synods or finance councils into deliberative rather than consultative bodies. None of them are colleges. They cannot place juridic collegial acts or indeed juridic acts of any kind and so while they could be said to form part of the post-conciliar development of 'co-responsibility' they lack the distinguishing marker of that which is canonically collegial (according to c. 115), which requires active participation in rendering decisions.

---

28.   See Beal, Coriden and Green, eds, *New Commentary*, 704.

In *CIC/17* moral persons, a forerunner in part of the juridical persons of *CIC* were divided into two types, collegial or non-collegial. However *CIC/17* gave no definition of 'collegial' and Gauthier says, canonists disagreed about its meaning in the old Code.[29] Since the first mention of 'collegial and 'college' in *CIC* appears in c. 115 and in a specific, juridic working context, it is worth looking closely at the messages they convey about both concepts.

Firstly, collegial decision making is participative and operates at a much higher level than simply advising or being consulted. It demands active participation in forming decisions which have juridic effect and through which the conduct of the college is determined. The original Latin of *CIC* is much clearer than any of the available translations in this regard '*si eius actionem determinant membra, in decisionibus ferendis concurrentia*'. Some translate this as making decisions, a phrase sometimes differentiated from taking decisions, suggesting one could contribute to a deliberative process (decision making) but someone else could take the decision. The Latin text makes no such distinction. It intends that members of a college guide its conduct by shared decision making and shared decision taking.

Secondly the status of collegial juridic personhood does not infer equality between group members with regard to status or power. For example within episcopal conferences there are differences in status, authority and power between auxiliary and other bishops.

Canon 119 deals with the conduct of the affairs of collegial juridic persons, including elections. It is the only occasion where *CIC* addresses how members of a collegial juridic person are to arrive at the collegial will. Such juridic persons, by their decision making processes, place, what are called 'collegial acts'. It is not explicit but is implied that the reference to 'collegial acts' is only to acts of collegial juridic persons. Reference to any broader class can only be by way of 'suggested analogy'.[30] So here again we get an informative insight into the nature of specifically collegial as opposed to non-collegial processes.

29.   See Albert Gauthier, 'Juridical Persons in the Code of Canon Law', *Studia Canonica*, 25 (1991): 85–7.
30.   See Beal, Coriden and Green, eds, *New Commentary*, 164.

Canon 119 could be regarded as setting out a basic default position for collegial acts in the absence of any superseding provisions in universal or particular laws or in the statutes of collegial juridic persons. It tends towards minimum standards rather than maximum and it has been pointed out that these days 'many collegial juridic persons ... would incorporate into their statutes, provisions ... that differ markedly from the provisions in the canon'.[31] Nonetheless the canon makes an important distinction between collegial acts which affect the members as individuals and collegial acts which do not. In the case of the latter, including elections there is an insistence on majority rule (and usually an absolute majority) except in exceptional circumstances. Lo Castro sees this as a considerable advance on *CIC/17* and a visible effort at balance by the legislator between the free-flow of 'collective responsibility' expressed through the will of the majority on the one hand and the efficient 'management of the entity on the other'.[32] However c. 119 §3 requires that 'what touches all as individuals must be approved by all.' This imposes a requirement for unanimity in certain circumstances and it has a long association with both Roman and Canon Law. It has had crucial limiting consequences and indeed pitfalls for episcopal conferences where the rights of individual members have sometimes impeded the development or implementation of a collegial will.

Canon 120 adds little to our understanding of 'college' or 'collegial' except to the extent that it acknowledges that, post-foundation, membership of a collegial juridic person may be reduced below three and where reduced to one, that single member has the power to act as the collegial juridic person. This is a logical consequence of creating the abstract construct that is a juridic person, though it has the quirky effect of allowing the acts of one animate person to be described as 'juridic collegial acts'.

In quite a number of references which follow on from c. 115 (including c. 127), the word 'college' is immediately followed by the words 'or group'.[33] The word 'group' as the wider of the two terms is the preferred terminology of the Eastern Rite Code of

---

31.   Ibid.
32.   See *Exegetical Commentary*, vol. 1, 780.
33.   *CIC*, cc. 127, 60, 165, 166, 169, 174, 175, 176, 177, 182 and 183.

1990 where it covers a wide variety of bodies both collegial and non-collegial and also includes the narrower sub-category of the juridic college. The contribution of c. 127 to the collegiality debate is to underline the importance for the validity of juridic acts of giving proper recognition to the rights of members of a college or group whose counsel or consent a superior may be required by law to obtain. Failure to obtain the appropriate consent or to consult properly invalidates the act. Beal et al. see the canon as applying only where a superior needs the consent or counsel of a subordinate.[34] It is essentially a brake on the power of a superior according to Michel Thériault who argues that it is designed to facilitate co-responsibility and wide participation in decision making.[35] Thériault is also of the view that while the canon talks of 'convocation' in fact remote consultation or voting such as teleconferencing, fax or email are acceptable nowadays.[36]

Canon 127 is another example of *CIC*'s due process procedures which protect the rights of members of colleges (among other groups) where they are entitled, by law, to be involved in making and taking decisions.

Canon 140 §2 deals with rules for avoiding clashes of competence where more than one person or members of a college have been delegated to undertake certain matters. It is at one level a relatively innocuous provision, easily glossed over but by some liberal extenuation it impacts on the delegation by Christ of supreme and full power over the universal church to the College of Bishops and how it was intended that it be exercised. Canon 140 §2 says that where there has been a delegation to a college that is a collegial juridic person, then the rules set out in c. 119, apply unless the terms of the mandate of delegation say otherwise. It is also clear that once the delegation is given the college members can go to work as a college. The mandate itself permits the college to get on with doing that which has been delegated. This is how the mandate from Christ to Peter and through him to the Pope operates. The Pope needs no further mandate beyond his assumption of the office of Pope. Contrast

---

34.   See Beal, Coriden and Green, eds, *New Commentary*, 181.
35.   See *Exegetical Commentary*, vol. 1, 809.
36.   Ibid., 810.

this with the same mandate given by Christ to the Apostolic College and through it to the College of Bishops which requires a green light from the Pope for its exercise. It has been given once in the past century.

Canon 166 is among a number of canons dealing with the rights and responsibilities of colleges/groups with regard to ecclesiastical offices especially where they have rights of presentation, election or postulation. They are almost entirely procedural and technical in nature and only a few are worth combing for attitudes to processes which involve colleges. Some are designed to ensure that a superior cannot ride roughshod over the members of a college by ignoring their right to be convoked (c. 166). Others provide reasonable time limits in the event of dilatoriness of a college in acting as it should, for example in filling an elected office (c. 165). Overall *CIC* seeks to afford college members every opportunity to participate in college proceedings, through insistence on due process and penalising via invalidity, any circumstances in which they are improperly overlooked. This is because the mind of the college is an important driver of college activities. It can only be derived through a transparent and fair process of deliberation by the members, not through a superior acting alone and looking into his own heart!

Miñambres says of c. 166 that it 'permits the discovery of a certain internal structure in those groups that act collegially'.[37] It involves a president with significant rights and responsibilities regarding college procedures for it is the president who convokes the college according to the norms of law and whose action or inaction can render an election valid or invalid. The president may or may not be *primus inter pares* although Miñambres, echoing the *Nota*, says the former is more typical of 'collegial proceedings' in the church.

A number of these canons establish that belonging to the college/group in the sense of provable membership is an important trigger for certain rights like voting or entitlement to be present, among others. Canon 169 states that in order for an election to be valid 'no one may be allowed to vote who does not belong to the college or group.' There is an emphasis here on maintaining

---

37.   See *Exegetical Commentary*, vol. 1, 969.

the integrity of the college/group that was absent under *CIC/17* where in certain circumstances outsiders, i.e. non members of the group or college could be permitted to vote. *CIC* takes a tougher line, so tough that a vote by an outsider renders any vote of the college/group invalid. The contamination of the vote of a college or group in such circumstances is taken very seriously and is punishable (c. 1375). It is worth commenting here in passing that the voting membership of an Ecumenical Council, can be wider than the College of Bishops (c. 339 §2) as indeed was the case at Vatican II.

Canon 173 provides for the scrutiny, collection and counting of votes in elections within a college/group. Drafted before the advent of teleconferencing and electronic voting it envisages the physical gathering of members in one place for voting and recording votes. Miñambres believes that c. 173 does not rule out the use of more modern election and voting systems.[38] Again what emerges from this canon is a concern to ensure that the voting rights of each member are treated with respect and that the will of the college or group is fairly and honestly assessed and recorded. This goes to internal collegial processes which need to be scrupulous in ensuring that no member's rights are overlooked or unfairly constrained and that college decisions flow from a process that is fully participatory.

Canon 174 provides for election by compromise, when a college or group unanimously and in writing, effectively delegates its electoral power to a person or persons, who may or may not be members of the college/group. Once again there is an emphasis on unanimity and on the certainty that comes from having full consent of the membership recorded in writing. In these requirements we see repeated concern for the rights of members of a college/group to have their say and to have traceable processes which protect and vindicate those rights.

Though Book Two is more important to the later discussion of conciliar collegiality, the procedural canon c. 699 sheds some additional light on the difference between collegial and non-collegial forms of decision making. Canon 699 concerns the final part of dismissal procedures for members of Religious

---

38.   Ibid., 989.

Institutes. It creates two separate procedures one collegial and
the other non-collegial. They are not alternates to one another.
They apply to different groups. The collegial process (which is
also governed by c. 119 §2) applies to members of monasteries
who have a major superior other than their own moderator; the
non-collegial process applies to autonomous monasteries which
do not. The latter by virtue of c. 615 are 'entrusted to the special
vigilance of the diocesan bishop'.

The collegial procedure under c. 699 §1 involves review of
evidence (gathered and presented by others), by a convoked
and deliberative group/council of at least four and possibly five
people, the supreme moderator among them, who while they do
not form a tribunal, are a quasi-tribunal. There is a personal assessment of the evidence by each individual council member, an
opportunity for team assessment through mutual debate and
deliberation and an equally weighted secret ballot of the council
members. Dismissal requires an absolute majority and though
taken by collegial decision, the decree is issued by the superior
general. The diffused nature of the institute and the several
tiers of 'management' structure involved allow for a degree of
distance between the subject of the dismissal case and those
deciding it.

Under the non-collegial procedure the diocesan bishop
makes the decision on dismissal having been presented with the
proofs and recommendation of the council and moderator/
superior of the member's institute. Morrissey says that 'In such
instances there is no question of a collegial vote. The bishop
alone makes the decision.'[39] Although there is nothing to prevent the bishop from privately seeking expertise in assessing the
weight of the evidence the net effect is that the due process
checks and balances under the non-collegial procedure are considerably reduced. The local and close-quarters nature of the relationships involved between the subject of the dismissal case
and the members of the council lessen the scope for arms-length
objectivity and enhance the risk of bias. That risk, may be somewhat mitigated but is not transcended by the involvement of the
bishop.

---

39.   See *Exegetical Commentary*, vol. II/2, 1877.

From a due process perspective there is a qualitative difference in these two processes which leaves members of autonomous monasteries who come under c. 699 §2 in a weaker position than those who do not. The collegial process set out in c. 699 §1 has the scope to be more rigorous, objective and scrupulous.

Book Five covers the management, administration, disposal and acquisition of the church's material goods and property.[40] Parishes and dioceses may have considerable property holdings in the broad sense of the word 'property', from cash to chattels from intellectual property to real estate. Generally the diocesan bishop exercises primary administrative control but he cannot do so untrammelled.

For reasons of prudence, accountability and efficiency, cc. 1277 and 1292 impose a legal obligation on a bishop, not to act alone in taking certain important decisions. Depending on the circumstances set out either in *CIC* or by the relevant Episcopal Conference, the bishop must at least hear the views and in some cases obtain the consent, of the diocesan finance council and college of consultors. The word 'college' only arises in these canons in speaking of the college of consultors but the processes of consultation and consent it mandates, have distinctly co-responsibility/collegial overtones and are similar to some of the checks and balances found in Book One on General Norms. These canons and others in this section while in part designed to alleviate the bishop's administrative burden are also designed to address the risks inherent in allowing one person to exercise unfettered power over serious matters which have considerable downstream consequences for the church. They are a bulwark of sorts against criminality, stupidity and rashness given that the property concerned does not belong to the bishop but is in his trust to be administered for the welfare of the diocese. The bishop's authority is cantilevered with the balance brought to his deliberations by the counsel or consent/refusal of the college of consultors and the finance committee. The church's caution in these matters is sensible and shows an explicit vigilance about the exercise of personal episcopal authority, albeit in very limited circumstances.

---

40.   Canons 1277 and 1292 are discussed here.

Book Seven concerns judicial processes.[41] The words 'colle-gial' and 'collegiate' appear interchangeably usually to distin-guish a collegial/collegiate tribunal (three or more members) from a non-collegial/collegiate tribunal (sole judge). At another level they reaffirm the concern seen elsewhere to provide for collegial rather than individual oversight of particularly serious matters (c. 1425). The more complex the case the more likely it is that it will require to be heard before a collegiate tribunal than by a sole judge. The opportunity for collegial discussion and de-liberation is given a high priority in such cases. Even where for good reason there can only be a sole judge, c. 1424 §4 says that where possible 'the sole judge should associate himself with an assessor and an auditor.' Such provisions aim at best practice and at a level of rigour designed to conduce more reliable and credible outcomes.

Canon 1426 §1 says that a collegiate tribunal is to proceed 'collegially' and that its decisions are to be based on majority voting. Grocholewski points out that 'collegially' in this canon 'has a different meaning from its meaning in several other canons'.[42] It has to be read in the light of c. 1609. Procedural col-legiality generally favours decisions based on convocation and majority or absolute majority vote. Once the decision is made, it becomes the vote of the entire collegiate/collegial body, with dissenters submitting to the will of the majority. The process set out in c. 1609 is somewhat different. Each member of the college of judges is expected to review the evidence alone in the first in-stance and bring to the convoked tribunal their pre-written con-clusions on the merits of the case (c. 1609 §2). These are disclosed and a discussion takes place (c. 1609 §3). Members can change their original opinions but where the tribunal reaches a decision that is not unanimous, a dissenting judge can insist that his min-ority conclusion be forwarded to an appellate tribunal in the event of an appeal (c. 1609 §4). This last provision came about as a result of a compromise during a controversy at the drafting stage. A plan to permit the automatic reference of lower tribunal

---

41.   The following canons use the words 'college', 'collegial', 'collegially' and 'collegiate'; cc. 1421, 1425*, 1426*, 1428, 1429, 1441, 1449, 1455, 1505, 1609*, 1610 and 1612. Only those asterisked are discussed here.

42.   See *Exegetical Commentary*, vol. IV/1, 751.

dissenting views to appellate tribunals met with opposition. This would have seriously undermined collegial integrity and so a compromise was reached which allowed for a dissenting view to be heard on appeal, but only where the holder of the view insisted.[43] Essentially he or she makes a decision whether to maintain the fullest collegial integrity of the lower court decision or not. There is no attempt made to reconcile this provision with the requirement of secrecy in c. 1609 §2. The tension is evident here between acknowledging the independence of each individual judge and the need to maintain the collegial integrity and stability of decisions made by majority vote.

These procedural canons, even allowing that many represent a default position, show that the basic procedural infrastructure of Canon Law (both before and after Vatican II) sees collegial processes in the following terms:

1. 'College' signifies a body of members acting together as a group.
2. Members actively participate in the decision making and decision taking which guides the group's activities.
3. A collegial mind or will is generally established by conjoint discussion followed by majority vote.
4. Unanimity is required where an issue affects a member's rights as an individual.
5. Equality among members is not a requirement.
6. A potential source of danger to the exercise of members' rights is perceived as coming from those who are heads or superiors. Consequently, their exercise of power is circumscribed to minimise the risk of abuse of power. They are subject to penalties, including invalidation of process, to ensure they do not circumvent or ignore members' rights to participate.
7. Decisions made without properly conducted input from the full membership are likely to have difficulties with validity.
8. The collegial will, because it is broadly based and consensual has an integrity that is compromised by the unlawful omission of voices that are entitled to be heard or by inclusion of non-members' views.
9. Modern communication methods such as teleconferencing, e-voting etc. are not ruled out.
10. Collegial entities require effective structures to protect the rights of members.

---

43.   See *Communicationes*, 2 (1979), 140.

11. The more complex or serious in its consequences a decision is, the more Canon Law favours a collegial approach.

12. Collegial processes are seen as a bulwark against the arbitrary, rash or corrupt use of authority and are a justifiable check even on the exercise of episcopal power.

13. Collegial processes are a legitimate form of burden-sharing, including in episcopal decision making.

3.5.1 Conciliar Collegiality

There is no solid consensus as to what constitutes conciliar collegiality. The labels of effective and affective collegiality and co-responsibility are applied but there can be areas of overlap. Effective collegiality describes the high juridic law-making status of the College of Bishops (acknowledged at Vatican II) and certain specific actions of the College of Cardinals concerning governance of the universal church (which long pre-date Vatican II). Affective collegiality generally applies to other conjoint activity at episcopal level though there is often terminological seepage to cover lower level ecclesial activities. Collaboration at sub-episcopal level or involving governance of particular churches is said by many commentators to be more properly called co-responsibility though confusingly it is often cited as evidence of the conciliar collegial spirit which promoted wider consultation at all levels in the church. The further the discussion of conciliar collegiality drifts from effective collegiality, the more it becomes a loose blanket term that is difficult to pin down. I have divided conciliar collegiality into two discussion areas, the first is collegiality and the People of God and the second, episcopal collegiality.

Book Two of CIC[44] is the main source for both, though there are relevant canons in Book One,[45] Book Three[46] and Book Seven.[47] Many of the canons important to collegiality[48] do not

---

44. The following canons of Book Two use the words 'college', 'collegial', 'collegially' or 'collegiate'; cc. 264, 272, 330*, 331*, 333*, 336*, 337*, 339*, 350, 351, 352*, 359*, 375*, 377, 382, 404, 413, 419, 421, 422, 430, 443, 485, 491, 494, 501, 502*, 505, 508, 509, 557 and 699. Only those asterisked are of interest for the purposes of this section.

45. See c. 129.

46. See cc. 749, 754, 756 and 782.

47. See c. 1404.

48. See cc. 204, 208, 209, 212, 228, 334, 338, 339, 341, 342, 343, 346, 347, 348, 360, 447–59, 460, 461, 466, 495 and 500.

use the words 'college', 'collegial', 'collegially' or 'collegiate' at all.

Book Two contains the heart of the provisions for conciliar collegiality. Almost one third of *CIC* is devoted to Book Two which gives an idea of its importance. It is here that the church as a communion is given its shape, here that the old hierarchical caste structures are flattened somewhat and here too that conciliar collegiality is given its voice to the extent that it is. These things occur within both a canonical as well as a theological context. The title of Book Two, 'The People of God', sets the scene for an expansive landscape and grand language in sharp contrast to the more prosaic procedural language of Book One. The *munus* of governance is subtly subsumed into this book. Two of its preoccupations are relevant to this thesis, firstly, the hierarchical governance structure of the church and secondly the participation in the *munus* of governance by the faithful. But these have to be understood as functioning within both a divinely instituted structure of governance and a communion which unites those who govern with the governed. Papal primacy, episcopal collegiality, the differentiated roles of members, the obedience to authority and the exercise of authority are all part of an intricate and unified phenomenon, the view of which was altered appreciably by *LG*. Dulles says that unlike Vatican I,

> Vatican II approached the question of papal primacy in the light
> of several other ecclesiological doctrines, such as the relative au
> tonomy of particular churches, the *communio* concept of the uni
> versal church and the collegiality of the bishops as agents of
> communion.[49]

Dulles points out that the Council fathers at Vatican I, while conscious that the Pope's power of governance was limited, were unable to 'specify any limiting principle'. This exposed the church to ridicule from without and uncertainty within and in response to those tensions at Vatican II there was 'the beginning of a reassertion of episcopal collegiality'.[50]

---

49.   Avery Robert Dulles, *The Catholicity of the Church* (Oxford: Clarendon
       Press, 1987), 137.
50.   See ibid., 136.

Dulles use of the word 'beginning' is quite deliberate and validates Örsy's point about the leavening or slow burn effect of Vatican II. The conciliar notion of *communio* along with episcopal collegiality set the context in which the Pope exercises his primatial power and the People of God contribute to the *munus* of governance to the extent that they do. Dulles says 'Rome is the centre, the principle of unity. There can be no centre without a circumference and no circumference without a centre.'[51] That web of interlocking relationships between the centre and the circumference informed the debate on conciliar collegiality. The alignment of those relationships into juridic consequences and structures posed considerable difficulties for the drafters of CIC who struggled but ultimately failed to bring anything like clarity to the matter. They simply did not have the tools to do so.

3.5.2 *Collegiality and the People of God*
Canon 204 has been described as the 'true backbone of the entire code'.[52] It states that those who are incorporated by baptism into the People of God participate, each in his or her own way, in the priestly, prophetic and kingly role of Christ (c. 204 §1). They are all thus co-responsible for the church's mission. However the roles and authority assigned to members of the People of God with regard to the three *munera* are sharply differentiated in various canons of the Code. 'In the church there is diversity of ministry but unity of mission.'[53] The ground for differentiation had been laid in Book One by c. 129, one of CIC's most important provisions for understanding the differences between the laity and those in sacred orders when it comes to participation in church governance.

Canon 129 provides that those who have received sacred orders are qualified for the power of divinely instituted governance (also called the power of jurisdiction) whereas laymen and women can 'cooperate' in the exercise of that power. Disagreement during drafting led to using 'cooperate' instead of 'participate' which had appeared in both the 1980 *Schema* and

---

51.   Ibid., 146.
52.   See *Exegetical Commentary*, vol. II/1, 141.
53.   See Vatican II, Decree on the Apostolate of Lay People *Apostolicam Actuositatem*, 2 in Flannery, 405.

the 1982 *Schema*. Canon 129 suggests that lay involvement in church governance is a function of ecclesiastical law while those in sacred orders govern by divine institution. Viani says there is an 'absence of interpretive consensus' with regard to this norm[54] for not only is this an area of fundamental disagreement but other provisions in *CIC* make contradictory provisions. Some canons permit the appointment of lay people to governance / deliberative roles alongside and identical to clerics, such as membership of the college of judges (c. 1421 §2) yet c. 274 says that only clerics can be appointed to offices which require the power of orders or of ecclesiastical governance.

Lombardia's description of the 'intentional imprecision'[55] of c. 129 could apply to c. 274 §1 which further confuses a vexed area. It is directly lifted from c. 118 of *CIC/17* but is not easily reconciled with *CIC* c. 129 §1 or *CIC* c. 228. It provokes conflicting views between those who argue that the laity by virtue of baptism may participate in the *munus* of governance as recognized in *LG* 33 and those who quote *LG* 10, 18, 21 and 24, in support of a juridic link between ordination and governance which excludes the laity from all but the most tenuous roles in governance and even then by concession rather than right.

These opposing perspectives which were the direct legacy of Vatican II caused the Code commission difficulty right up to the last minute of the drafting process and much of the commission's final plenary meeting was devoted to sorting out the problems. The commission accepted for example that lay people could become tribunal judges, a governance role legitimated by papal authority and *LG*. Among the papers they considered was one from then Cardinal Ratzinger in which he objected to lay participation in governance, pointing out the contradiction between basing governance on sacred orders and yet allowing 'participation' by the laity.[56] The contradiction remains built in. As Beal et

---

54. See *Exegetical Commentary*, vol. 1, 821.
55. See Pedro Lombardia Diaz, *Lecciones De Derecho Canonico: Introduccion Derecho Constitucional, Parte General (Spanish Edition)* (Madrid: Grupo Anaya Comercial, 1984). I have used Viani's translation from the *Exegetical Commentary of Canon Law*, vol. 1, 821.
56. See *Pontificia Commissio Codicis Iuris Canonici Recognocendo*, Pontifical Commission for the Revision of the Code of Canon Law, Plenary Session, 20–9 October 1981, 35–87.

al. remark, 'there is no commonly accepted theological explanation for lay ministry.'[57]

Canon 204 §1, like LG[58] acknowledges that all Christ's faithful share in their own way in the three *munera* by virtue of their baptism. This poses questions which are as much theological as canonical and which impact on the meaning of c. 129. LG[59] encouraged greater involvement of the laity in the full mission of the church and bearing in mind the interpretive authority of the Council and the pressure towards greater lay participation in church management (provided for in c. 517 §2) arising out of the collapse in western vocations to the priesthood, the question concerning the exercise of the power of governance by the laity is still being debated.

It is important to bear in mind however the logistical realities of a universal church whose adherents comprise one sixth of the world's population, with some 400,000 parishes or missions and over 4,000 bishops. How is meaningful participation by the People of God in governance to be effected? According to Paul VI 'all members of the church are obligated to recognise the demands of a legal system; if this should fail, the *communio* in Christ could not be put into effect in social terms, nor could it function effectively.'[60] While this implies obedience of the faithful to the law it is clear that Vatican II envisaged more than the Vatican I model summarised a little cynically as 'pay, pray and obey'. Speaking of the laity, in particular, the Decree *Apostolicam Actuositatem* says 'Present circumstances, in fact, demand from them a more extensive and more vigorous apostolate.'[61] It goes on to say that the laity

> ... should develop the habit of working in the parish in close
> cooperation with their priests, of bringing before the ecclesial
> community their own problems, world problems and questions

---

57.   See Beal, Coriden and Green, eds, *New Commentary on the Code of Canon Law*, 348.

58.   See *LG*, 9–17, 31, 34–6 in Flannery, 12–25, 48–9 and 52–6.

59.   See ibid., 37 in Flannery, 56–7.

60.   See Paul VI, 'Discorso Ai Partecipanti', *Persona e Ordinamento nella Chiesa. Atti del II Congreso Internaziolale di Diritto Canonico. Milano 10–16 Settembre 1973 in L'Osservatore Romano, September 17–18, 1973.*

61.   See Vatican II, Decree on the Apostolate of Lay People *Apostolicam Actuositatem*, Introduction in Flannery, 403.

regarding humanity's salvation, to examine them together and solve them by general discussion.[62]

Beal et al. remark that this canon 'refers more explicitly to participation in the offices of priest and prophet, less explicitly to the governing office'.[63] This muted tone when it comes to participation in governance by the laity is hardly surprising in a church still resistant, as we will see, to fuller participation in governance by the College of Bishops whose authority is unequivocally acknowledged to be of divine origin.

Canon 204 §2 is much more explicit about the governance role of the Pope and the bishops and it marks a key dividing line. It describes the church as a society governed by 'the successor of Peter and the bishops in communion with him'. Fornés explains that by virtue of the institutional principle

> ... there exist in the church certain functions whose origin does not reside in the Christian people, but rather which have been assigned and granted directly by Christ to the hierarchy, i.e., the Roman Pontiff and the bishops together in communion with him.[64]

While, therefore, the People of God are implicated in some undefined way in the *munus* of governance, the Pope and the bishops have certain specific functions of governance given by Christ to them alone. In a further refinement as we will see later, the Pope's functions are much more clearly defined than those of the other bishops.

Differentiated functions and powers notwithstanding, c. 208 acknowledges the fundamental equality of all the faithful in terms of dignity and action, from which stems their involvement in 'building up the Body of Christ' according to the condition, function or office of each one. This is a major change from *CIC*/17 which saw the church in terms of superiors (clergy) who laid down the law and inferiors (laity), who obeyed. Fornés says that under *CIC*/17 'a class-based vision prevailed' which blurred the radical equality of the faithful, now reclaimed in *LG* and *CIC*.[65] The equality that is acknowledged is limited by the different

---

62.   Ibid., 10 in Flannery, 417.
63.   See Beal, Coriden and Green eds, *New Commentary*, 247.
64.   See *Exegetical Commentary*, vol. II/1, 20.
65.   Ibid., 3.

classes of contribution made by members to the work of the
church and very different rights. This canon which echoes *LG*[66]
provides for potentially the greatest disconnect between the pre
and post-conciliar church but as has been pointed out 'difficulties remain in the activation of this participation: adequate
structures are not always available to encourage dynamic involvement of the faithful; and some of the faithful remain unaware of their obligations in this regard'.[67] Fornés urges a degree of caution in over-inflating the expectations created by this
canon, agreeing with Herranz that it is neither a promise of democratic structures and processes, nor is it correct to describe it
as a form of collegiality.[68] It is nothing more or less than the
principle of co-responsibility of all the faithful to which each
contributes according to their differentiated roles. This view is
echoed in two Post Synodal Apostolic Exhortations, *Pastores
gregis*[69] (on bishops) and *Christifideles laici* (on the laity). In the
case of the latter the sole mention of collegiality is in relation to
the Pope's assertion that his apostolic exhortation is the 'fruit of
collegiality' between himself and the Synod.[70]

Canon 208 is followed by fifteen canons sometimes characterised rather fancifully as a charter of fundamental rights and
obligations of the faithful. They mostly derive from the *Schema
postremum* of the *Lex Ecclesiae Fundamentalis* (1980) (*LEF*), an
aborted attempt at drafting a church constitution. Parts of *LEF*
were subsumed into *CIC* though the word 'fundamental' was
dropped for fear of raising parallels with the much more radical
meaning of fundamental rights in the secular sphere.

Canon 209 sets the scene. The faithful are to maintain communion with the church. Ghirlanda has described this as the
primary duty of all the faithful.[71] When c. 212 expresses what

---

66.   See *LG*, 32 in Flannery, 49–51.
67.   See Beal, Coriden and Green, eds, *New Commentary*, 258.
68.   See *Exegetical Commentary*, vol. II/1, 39.
69.   See John Paul II, Apostolic Exhortation *Pastores Gregis* (16 October 2003) in
      AAS, 96 (2004), 825–924.
70.   See post-Synodal apostolic exhortation on the mission and vocation of
      the lay faithful *Christifideles Laici*. 30 December 1988 in *AAS*, 81 (1989),
      393–521.
71.   See Gianfranco Ghirlanda, 'Doveri E Diritti Dei Fedeli Nella Communione
      Ecclesiale', *La Civilita Cattolica* 136, no. 1 (1985): 24.

Beal et al. call 'the dynamic nature of the church as commu-nion'[72] in reality the dynamic is well circumscribed. The faithful are to be obedient to the teaching of their pastors (c. 212 §1) and though they have the right to make their needs and desires known to their pastors (c. 212 §2), and the right (even the duty) according to c. 212 §3 to make their opinions known to their pas-tors or the rest of the church, they are only permitted to do so where it is 'without prejudice to the integrity of faith and morals'. These provisions remain largely unknown and unused. There are no standing structures designed to give effect to them though diocesan Synods have a specific obligation to ascertain the desires of the faithful with regard to the Synod agenda. The actual agenda is decided by the bishop.[73]

Canon 228 allows that members of the laity, by virtue of their skills or qualifications may be capable of performing certain roles in the *munus* of governance. It is not an expression of a right for there is no such right as we saw in c. 129. It is an ac-knowledgment of capability and as such an advance on *CIC/17*. *CIC* makes limited provision for lay cooperation in church gov-ernance. Laity can be members of pastoral councils (c. 512), fin-ance councils (c. 492), diocesan synods (c. 463), particular coun-cils (c. 443), holders of ecclesiastical offices (c. 228 §1), judges in tribunals (c. 1421), defenders of the bond (c. 1435) and expert ad-visors (c. 228 §2). In practical terms this means that at universal church level a small number of laity now work in some dicaster-ies and tribunals. At national and diocesan level there is greater lay involvement in pastoral and diocesan councils, finance com-mittees, church tribunals and in parish and diocesan administ-ration. Lay experts contribute nationally and internationally to the interface between the church and civic society through in-volvement in church bodies such as, for example in Ireland, Social Welfare, Justice and Peace, Emigrants, Prisoners Abroad and Child Protection etc.

While such fora encourage active participation in church life, enhance the contribution made by the church to civic society,

---

72.   See Beal, Coriden and Green eds, *New Commentary*, 263.
73.   See Congregation for Bishops and Congregation for the Evangelisation of Peoples, 'Instructions on Diocesan Synods', 8 July 1997 in *AAS*, 89 (1997), 706–21.

and even help guide the direction of local practice or policy they lack juridic powers of decision making, involve statistically insignificant percentages and make a negligible contribution to universal church teaching. In the early 1980s the Irish Catholic Church's Commission on Social Welfare (which had a lay majority) was instrumental in persuading the Irish Bishops to support governmental abolition of the status of illegitimacy. By contrast, two areas of widespread non-compliance with church teaching in the developed world, confession and family planning, have never been formally discussed below episcopal level. BASIC, an Irish organisation which advocates the admission of women to the priesthood, claims that both the Primate of All-Ireland and the Papal Nuncio declined to accept letters from it which showed the level of support among the faithful for women priests.[74] This indicates the constraints on the right and duty enunciated in c. 212 §3. In the absence of formal facilitation of free-ranging discussion within the church, lively debates among the faithful are largely conducted in the secular space, in newspapers, journals, conferences, radio, television and the internet, with their wide arena for uncensored discussion. The contrast with the lack of in-church structures creates its own problems as does the impression, created by default, that the church is always under attack from without.

Such lay involvement as exists in church governance, is quite marginal and varies greatly from place to place. It may derive from the conciliar desire for more lay participation in church life but it is debatable whether it expresses conciliar collegiality. This story is evolving, for just as a dearth of priests in mission territories saw more work devolve to the laity, a similar dearth in parts of the western world has forced increased levels of lay involvement. The juridic consequences of these changes are far from fleshed out yet.

3.5.3 *Episcopal Collegiality*
In cc. 330–41 the ambiguous conciliar views on episcopal colleg - iality, come forcibly into play. The imprint of *LG* is evident throughout. *CIC*'s provisions in relation to supreme governance

---

74.   See www.basic.ie, Petition. [Accessed 22.3.2009.]

of the church are placed, as in *LG*, within the broader context of the People of God. Amidst considerable confusion one subject seems settled, that the supreme governance structure of the church is of divine institution whether the subject is the Pope or the College of Bishops. The supreme authority of the church derives its legitimacy from Christ through the apostles including Peter (*LG* 22). Oakley[75] and others have pointed out and *LG* acknowledges that supreme governance methodologies have changed from age to age. Vatican I asserted the primatial authority of the Pope. His full and supreme power of governance was fully authenticated by Vatican II and is expressed in *CIC* (cc. 331, 332 and 333). However *LG* made the following significant changes to universal church governance which are found in the provisions of *CIC*.

(a) The formal juridic recognition for the first time of the concept the College of Bishops (c. 330).

(b) The assertion of the College's full and supreme power of governance over the universal church (with the College's Head who is the Pope [cc. 331 and 336] and never without its Head).

(c) The acceptance that the powers of the College of Bishops could be exercised outside of an Ecumenical Council (c. 337).

We saw above in discussing *LG* that the word 'college' was so problematic that the *Nota* made the following clarifications.

(a) The College of Bishops is not a college of equals in the strict juridic sense, and has a non-juridical, purely pastoral meaning.[76]

(b) Any exercise of powers of governance by the College of Bishops requires Papal authorisation. 'The Roman Pontiff undertakes the regulation, encouragement and approval of the exercise of collegiality as he sees fit, having regard to the church's good' (*Nota* 3).[77] *CIC* expresses this in c. 337 §3.

(c) The College of Bishops is always in existence but it is not 'continually engaged in strictly collegiate activity' (*Nota* 4).[78]

(d) The college cannot act independently of the Pope. 'In default of the Pope's action, the bishops cannot act as a college …

---

75.   See Francis Oakley, *The Conciliarist Tradition: Constitutionalism in the Catholic Church, 1300–1870*, 76–87.

76.   See Beal, Coriden and Green, eds, *New Commentary*, 423.

77.   See *LG* in Flannery, 94.

78.   Ibid.

This hierarchical communion of all bishops with the Pope is unmistakably hallowed by tradition' (*Nota* 4).[79]

(e) Without hierarchical communion the 'sacramental-ontological' office cannot be exercised but this is without prejudice to the canonical-juridical issues of validity and liceity which were left to the deliberations of theologians (*Nota* 4).[80]

Canons 330–41 deal with the roles of the Pope and the College of Bishops. The territory is theological and what is astonishing for an institution now two millennia old, is the extent to which these roles are today incapable of unequivocal articulation. Beal et al. remark that it has been historically difficult 'to agree a convincing boundary between an acceptable centralised function of the primacy and an oppressive papal centralism'.[81] The Council found the best solution it could, even if there are demonstrable 'weaknesses, loopholes and ambivalence in the council's ecclesiology'.[82] Those problems had to be worked through by the Code commission but with their hands tied by the Council. The gravitational pull of primatialism over conciliarism / collegiality is apparent in the provisions of *CIC* but since both had to be accommodated there is evidence of a complex and incomplete vision of both collegiality and *communio*. The Code commission was unable to bring both concepts fully home and so, unsurprisingly, this section of the Code provokes contradictory commentaries.

3.6 The Pope

An important clarification was made in c. 330 which affirmed that the Pope was a member of the College of Bishops and not separate from the college. *CIC*/17 had made no mention of the college nor as a consequence of the Pope as its Head, so this was new territory for the Code commission. The formula it uses, 'Peter and the rest of the apostles form one college', was insisted upon by Cardinal Alfrink because it avoided the much more problematic formula 'Peter and the apostles' which could be interpreted as two separate strands. The entire canon was absent

---

79. Ibid.
80. Ibid., 94–5.
81. See Beal, Coriden and Green, eds, *New Commentary*, 425.
82. Ibid.

from all but the final draft and was in fact inserted very late in the drafting process. It is not to be found in the *Lex Fundamentalis* yet if ever there was a fundamental constitutional position this must surely qualify, indeed it is the lead canon in this pivotal section. Molano says that it gives 'the entire chapter a strong collegial emphasis in keeping with Vatican II',[83] for while Peter is placed at the head of the apostles he is not outside of them. He adds that it is clear that

> ... if the college were not the subject of full and supreme power, the power of the Roman Pontiff would be diminished when he acts as the Head of the College in strictly collegiate activity, because the college cannot exist without its Head. The Pope would only enjoy full power when acting personally and not collegially.[84]

This is not a college of equals according to the *Nota*. The subordination of the other bishops to the Pope is repeatedly emphasised in this and other canons, although c. 333 §2 says that the Pope 'is always joined in full communion with the other bishops and indeed the whole church'. The absence of a specific legal structure to give effect to this 'communion' has been described as one of the code's 'central weaknesses'.[85] It negates the *Nota*'s assurance that communion 'is not to be understood as some vague sort of goodwill but as something organic which calls for a juridical structure' (*Nota* 2).[86]

Beal et al. say that the upshot of c. 333 §2 is that 'papal decisions and actions that do not agree with the conviction of the bishops and the ecclesial community are unthinkable and impossible, at least from a moral point of view.'[87] The final part of that sentence is worth pondering. From a legal point of view there is no mechanism in the Code for overruling a papal decision. Canon 333 §3 says that all judgments and decrees of the Pope are subject to neither appeal nor recourse. While not everything the Pope does or says constitutes a decree or a judgement, c. 1404 creates a much wider net of impunity and

---

83.   See *Exegetical Commentary*, vol. II / 1, 588.
84.   Ibid., 611.
85.   See Beal, Coriden and Green, eds, *New Commentary*, 440.
86.   See *LG* in Flannery, 93.
87.   See Beal, Coriden and Green, eds, *New Commentary*, 426.

unaccountability when it says simply that 'the Holy See is judged by no-one'. With no mechanism to challenge the Pope juridically the court of public opinion (where Canon Law holds no sway) has become the lightning rod for debate and dissent and an informal accountability mechanism. Public dismay expressed through the media (including by some Cardinals) has caused Pope Benedict XVI to apologise or change his mind on a number of occasions.

The Pope's 'pre-eminent ordinary power over all particular churches' is acknowledged (c. 333 §1) as is his right to decide in the light of the needs of the church whether to exercise his role as Supreme Pastor collegially or personally (c. 333 §3). This seems to answer, at least in part, a criticism made by Lakeland of *LG* that 'it never makes it entirely clear whether collegiality is in service of primacy or primacy in service of collegiality.'[88] It is absolutely clear here that the collegial exercise of papal authority is a matter for the Pope based on his own assessment of the needs of the church.

According to c. 230 of *CIC/17*, the Cardinals were said to 'constitute a Senate of the Roman Pontiff and are the principal counsellor to him in governing the church and the helpers who assist him'.[89] The 'Senate' status of the College of Cardinals is not repeated in *CIC*. Instead c. 334 says the bishops are available to cooperate with the Pope in a number of ways including the Synod of Bishops. It further provides that the Cardinals and other persons and institutes may assist him as circumstance and the law require. According to Beal et al. this considerably extends the range of collegial options open to the Pope and clarifies the ways in which the Pope may act collegially which includes the assistance he gets from the Curia.[90]

Molano views c. 334 differently, arguing that it is concerned exclusively with the personal exercise of the Pope's power and not its collegial exercise,[91] a view he claims is supported by the *Communicationes*.[92] He believes the Pope's personal exercise of

88.   See Mannion, *The Vision of John Paul II: Assessing His Thought and Influence*, 190.
89.   See Peters, ed., *CIC/17*, 96.
90.   See Beal, Coriden and Green, eds, *New Commentary*, 442.
91.   See *Exegetical Commentary*, vol. II/1, 640.
92.   See *Communicationes*, 8 (1976), 99.

pastoral jurisdiction can enter 'the field of collegiality in a broad sense and it could easily be described as collegial cooperation.' If Molano is right the Pope acts collegially with the Cardinals when they are acting collectively as the College of Cardinals but in his interaction with individual Cardinals he is acting personally though in the broad field of collegial cooperation. Molano does make the point that in these canons 'the lines between personal and collegial governance are very fluid' and that they can be read as supporting both primatialism and collegiality.[93]

Regardless of whether c. 334 is designed to assist the Pope in exercising his office collegially or personally, its open-ended nature does allow the Pope wide scope to create consultative or advisory bodies or to seek help from individuals or institutes far beyond what was provided for under *CIC/17*. This can be seen as opening up the papacy to a greater range of opinion and advice or it can equally be seen as consolidating centralisation and primatialism since all choices in the matter remain with the Pope.

Canon 331 looks like a classic statement of primatialism, listing the many papal titles, offices, powers and impunity. He is Bishop of the Roman Church, Head of the College of Bishops, Vicar of Christ, Pastor of the universal church on earth, possessor of supreme, full, immediate and universal ordinary power, 'which he is always able to exercise freely'. Beal et al. say that while individually the elements of the list are not new (apart from Head of the College of Bishops), 'In the context of a juridical description of collegiality, the combination suggests a definition of the primacy unlike any other known in the history of Canon Law.'[94]

The description of the Pope's powers as 'supreme, full, immediate and universal' is a marked change from *CIC/17* which afforded the Pope 'supreme and full power' (c. 218) and afforded the Ecumenical Council 'supreme' power (c. 228). The four adjectives 'supreme', 'full', 'immediate' and 'universal', first appeared in the 1980 version of the *Lex Fundamentalis* drawing on the anxiety evident in *LG* 22 to protect primatialism even while providing for episcopal collegiality. Both the Pope and the College of Bishops possess infallibility (c. 749) in similar terms,

---

93.   *Exegetical Commentary*, vol. II / 1, 586–7.
94.   See Beal, Coriden and Green, eds, *New Commentary*, 431.

but the words 'immediate and universal' are not used to describe the 'full and supreme power' of the College of Bishops (c. 336). Inexplicably c. 332 which describes how the Pope qualifies for his power, speaks only of his 'full and supreme power' (exactly the same expression used for the College of Bishops) and makes no mention of the words 'immediate and universal'.

Responding to criticism of primatialism, Pope John Paul II in the encyclical *Ut Unum Sint* invited those inside and outside the church to participate in a dialogue to help 'find a way of exercising the primacy which, while in no way renouncing what is essential to its mission, is nonetheless open to a new situation'.[95] Responding to that invitation the Congregation for the Doctrine of the Faith (whose head was then Cardinal Ratzinger) published its *'Reflections on the Primacy of Peter'* in 1998:

> The primatial office of the Bishop of Rome and the office of the other bishops are not in opposition but in fundamental and essential harmony. Therefore, 'The episcopacy and the primacy, reciprocally related and inseparable, are of divine institution ... when the Catholic Church affirms that the office of the Bishop of Rome corresponds to the will of Christ, she does not separate this office from the mission entrusted to the whole body of bishops, who are also "vicars and ambassadors of Christ" (*LG* 27). The Bishop of Rome is a member of the "college", and the bishops are his brothers in the ministry.' It should also be said, reciprocally, that episcopal collegiality does not stand in opposition to the personal exercise of the primacy nor should it relativise it ... This does not mean, however, that the Pope has absolute power. Listening to what the churches are saying is, in fact, an earmark of the ministry of unity, a consequence also of the unity of the episcopal body and of the *sensus fidei* of the entire People of God.[96]

The reflections make little contribution to 'a new situation' for they simply restate the same conciliar obfuscations which failed to fully describe the constitutional relationship between the Pope's primatial powers and his Headship of the College of Bishops, and failed to give episcopal collegiality a clearly defined role.

95.   See John Paul II, encyclical letter *Ut unum sint*, no. 95.
96.   Congregation for the Doctrine of the Faith, *Il Primato del Successore di Pietro*, Atti del Simposio Teologico, Rome, 2–4 December 1996, Libreria Editrice Vaticana, Vatican City, 1998, English translation in Origins, 28, 1998–1999, 207–16.

The most comprehensive contemporary exposition of the Pope's powers of governance vis-à-vis the College of Bishops is to be found in the *motu proprio* of John Paul II *Apostolos Suos* (*ApS*) which in clarifying the theological and canonical status of episcopal conferences has much to say on the subject of episcopal collegiality:

> In the universal communion of the People of God, for the service of which the Lord instituted the apostolic ministry, the collegial union of bishops shows forth the nature of the church. Just as the church is one and universal, so also is the episcopacy one and indivisible, extending as far as the visible structure of the church and expressing her rich variety. The visible source and foundation of this unity is the Roman Pontiff, the head of the episcopal body.
>
> Collegially, the order of Bishops is, 'together with its head, the Roman Pontiff, and never without this head, the subject of supreme and full power over the universal church.' As it is well known, in teaching this doctrine, the Second Vatican Council likewise noted that the Successor of Peter fully retains 'his power of primacy over all, pastors as well as the general faithful. For in virtue of his office, that is, as Vicar of Christ and pastor of the whole church, the Roman Pontiff has full, supreme and universal power over the church. And he can always exercise this power freely' (*ApS* Arts 8–9).[97]

It still remains unclear however after Vatican II, *CIC* and numerous documents and debates whether the Pope has one or two strands of divinely instituted authority. Is his primatial authority derived exclusively from Christ through his Headship of the College of Bishops (the apostles including Peter their Christ-chosen leader) or is there an overarching additional strand of authority deriving directly from Christ through Peter to the Pope?

3.7 The College of Bishops
If *CIC* defines primacy anew it is equally true that it redefines the College of Bishops. The redefinition is problematic: it straddles two contexts, the new and poorly articulated context of conciliar episcopal collegiality and the old, well-established context of primatialism. However, it clearly avers the governmental authority of the College of Bishops over the universal

---

97.   John Paul II, Apostolic Letter *Apostolos Suos* in *AAS* 90 (1998), 641–58.

church and its ability to render infallible decisions or statements both inside and outside Ecumenical Councils (cc. 336 and 749 § 2). Lash says that the need:

> … to balance due recognition of papal primacy with acknowl-edgement that every bishop is, in his church, 'vicar and ambas-sador of Christ' (LG 27) and that it is the College of Bishops, led by the Bishop of Rome, which is the governing body of the Catholic Church was generally agreed to be at the heart and cen-tre of the council's programme.[98]

While c. 336 reiterates c. 331's description of the Pope as the Head of the College of Bishops, it states (for the first time in Canon Law) that the College of Bishops (with its Head the Pope and never without its Head) has 'supreme and full power over the universal church' (c. 336). CIC/17 had recognised only the Pope (c. 219) and the Ecumenical Council (c. 228) as having such full legislative jurisdiction over the universal church (though the College of Cardinals had limited and highly circumscribed powers in a Vacant See). Beal et al. say of c. 336 that it 'must be the one canon of the code that gives rise to the largest number of difficulties in interpretation'.[99] Molano sees it as 'the key for in-terpreting other canons of the Code related to the principle of collegiality'.[100] The Code commission in drafting this canon had 'no prior model in the history of Canon Law'[101] to offer help or guidance. The text went through many permutations drawing heavily mostly on LG, and the Nota as well as Christus Dominus and Ad Gentes but in the end it simply became a recipe for ongo-ing dispute between two main schools of thought, one of which is that it is the college with its Head which has full and supreme power over the church while the other says both the Pope and the College of Bishops have full and supreme power. Both are poorly distinguished. Molano and Lakeland conclude that the Code if anything consolidates primatialism.

Beal et al. dispute the legitimacy of insisting that the College of Bishops cannot have full and supreme power without its Head arguing that 'This does not agree with historical facts,

---

98.   Nicholas Lash, 'Could the Shutters yet Come Down?', 13.
99.   See Beal, Coriden and Green eds, New Commentary, 444.
100.   See Exegetical Commentary, vol. II/1, 610.
101.   See Beal, Coriden and Green eds, New Commentary, 444.

with the very notion of a college, or with the teachings of the legitimate ecumenical councils of Constance and Basle.'[102] If they
are correct then not only does *CIC* not advance the position of
the College of Bishops but it may have actively conspired to its
dilution. Their view is vindicated by the canons which follow.
The College of Bishops exercises its power over the universal
church 'in solemn form' in Ecumenical Councils (c. 337 §1). That
same power can also be exercised outside of the Council by the
'united action of the bishops dispersed throughout the world'
provided that the Pope has publicly declared or freely accepted
such an exercise of power 'so that it becomes a true collegial act'
(c. 337 §2). Beal et al. say the provisions of c. 337 §2 were designed with the rare possibility of epistolary councils in mind.[103]
The provision is lifted word for word from *LG* 22 and was the
subject of some doubt on the part of the Code commission. It
was thought to cover such an unlikely occurrence that to provide for it was unnecessary, particularly in the light of c. 337 §3
(discussed below) which provides that the Pope is to decide the
ways in which the College of Bishops may act collegially with
regard to the universal church 'according to the needs of the
church'. In the end though the provision was included and on
the face of it c. 337 §2 seems to provide for ex *post facto* ratification by the Pope of initiatives generated from within the
College of Bishops but not specifically initiated by the Pope, for
which there is some historical precedent, a view also endorsed
in *ApS* Art 9. Interestingly c. 337 §2 is not expressly made subject
to 337 §3, but all acts of governance by the College of Bishops do
require papal approval to render them valid.

> The supreme power which the body of bishops possesses over
> the whole church cannot be exercised by them except colleg-
> ially, either in a solemn way when they gather together in ecu-
> menical Council, or spread throughout the world, provided that
> the Roman Pontiff calls them to act collegially or at least freely
> accepts their joint action.

The possibility of extra-conciliar governance by the College of
Bishops is enhanced by analogy with c. 440 where it is possible

---

102.   Ibid., 424.
103.   Ibid., 448.

to have retrospective ratification by a newly elected Pope of decisions of a Council juridically ended by the death of a Pope.

Whether or not the College of Bishops can initiate actions without its Head, the Pope controls the validity of such acts and so remains in effective control of all forms of episcopal collegial action inside and outside Ecumenical Councils. This extension of primatial powers is particularly significant in light of the changes to Ecumenical Councils under *CIC*. *CIC/17* devoted an entire chapter to Ecumenical Councils. They don't merit a sub-heading in *CIC* where they constitute the solemn form (among other forms) of universal governance exercised by the College of Bishops (c. 336 §1). Their once 'supreme power' (*CIC/17* c. 228) is not replicated in *CIC*. According to Beal et al. the former juridical position

> … of the ecumenical council has been extensively neutralised by the integration of the council under the superior notion of 'college of bishops,' and by its inclusion in a series of possible means of collegial action. Thus in the light of this legal position one can ask whether or not it is even necessary for an ecumenical council ever to take place again.[104]

Given that the number of bishops worldwide has almost doubled since Vatican II, the logistics of extended physical convocation, of the universal episcopate, adds force to the view that in its old format, an Ecumenical Council could be a thing of the past. If that is so and in the absence of new ways for the College of Bishops to act as a legislative force, it is easy to comprehend why some query if anything has changed in terms of universal church governance practice since Vatican II or *CIC*. The Pope continues to exercise day-to-day control of the church to the same extent as before Vatican II. No standing mechanism exists to facilitate the exercise by College of Bishops of its power of governance. There is some consultation/ communication between the Pope and individual members or groupings of members of the College of Bishops e.g. the Synod of Bishops, College of Cardinals, *ad limina* visits, Episcopal Conferences and the Curia, but none is legally representative of the College of

---

104.   Ibid.

Bishops. The Synod of Bishops[105] and the College of Cardinals[106] have from time to time as we will see, been described as representing the College of Bishops but 'representative' in what sense? Their membership is drawn from the episcopacy and can only be drawn canonically from the college but they are 'representative' only in a colloquial and not a constitutional/legal sense. Their reporting relationship is to the Pope and not to the body they are said to represent, that is the College of Bishops. In fact as we shall see later *CIC* carefully avoids any explicit suggestion of a juridic link between the College of Bishops and either the Synod of Bishops or the College of Cardinals. While papal interaction with bodies such as the Synod, College of Cardinals, Episcopal Conferences and the Curia, provides greater post-Conciliar consultative diversity (c. 334), it operates from a jurido/constitutional platform which is much clearer about primatialism than it is about episcopal collegiality. The relationship of such bodies with the Pope is well articulated while their constitutional/juridic relationship with the College of Bishops is not.

Vatican II was unable to decide whether the powers of the College of Bishops could be delegated either partially or fully.[107] *ApS* comes close to saying they cannot. 'The individual bishops, as teachers of the faith, do not address the universal community of the faithful except through the action of the entire College of Bishops.'[108] For as long as that question remains open it imposes a brake on the development of a truly juridically representative role by bodies such as the Synod of Bishops, the College of Cardinals or any other body which might be delegated, whether fully or by limited mandate, by the College of Bishops to share universal governance power on its behalf with the Pope, *cum et sub Petro*.

---

105. See Homily of Pope John Paul II at the Conclusion of the Synod Of Bishops, 27 October 2001, www.vatican.va/holy_father/john_ paul_ii/ homilies/2001/documents/hf_jpii_hom_20011027_closing-synod_en.html. [Accessed 01.10.2008.]

106. See Beal, Coriden and Green, eds, *New Commentary*, 448.

107. See Alberigo and Komonchak, eds, *History of Vatican II: Mature Council*, 67.

108. See John Paul II, Apostolic Letter *Apostolos Suos*, 11.

The Pope's power of governance is free-flowing and active
from the moment he becomes Pope. The College of Bishops is
not. Although it subsists by divine law it can only be activated
by the Pope. Of the nine twentieth century Popes, John XXIII
alone exercised that power by inaugurating an Ecumenical
Council: Paul VI exercised it by continuing and completing the
Council. No Pope since Vatican II has facilitated active participation in universal church governance by the College of
Bishops. With some notable exceptions, members of the
College of Bishops have remained silent on the subject. It has
been discussed at the Synod of Bishops but without significant
recommendations on the matter. It seems odd that the divinely-
ordained College of Bishops cannot place collegial acts during a
vacant or impeded See while a juridically 'inferior' body, the
College of Cardinals can, as it does when it elects a Pope or takes
over the care and maintenance of the church in an interregnum.
The fact remains that a collegial body of such import as the
College of Bishops has made no post-conciliar contribution to
church governance except in the extenuated sense that the Pope
can claim to have made decisions as Head of the College,
though without ever formally consulting the college.

As a body the College of Bishops has since Vatican II acted
collegially only in the sense of maintaining *communio* through
passive obedience to the Pope. Cardinal Kasper has asked
rhetorically whether the authority and initiative of the College
of Bishops has not been reduced to a 'naked fiction' when the
Head of the College can and does always act without the formal
involvement of the college?[109] Eschenburg takes the argument
back to the Council where he believes that despite claims about
progress in episcopal collegiality, the relationship between
papal power and the power of the College of Bishops remained
the same as Vatican I.[110] The difference between the two
Councils is that Vatican II created the potential for change, a

---

109.   See Walter Kasper, 'Zur Theologie und Praxis des Bischöflichen Amtes' in
       Auf neue Art Kirche Sein: Wirklichkeiten–Herausfoderungen–Wandlungen,
       Werner Schreer and Georg Steins eds (Munich: Bernward bei Don Bosco,
       1999), 43.
110.   See T. Eschenberg, *Über autorität* (Frankfurt, Suhrkamp, 1976), 35.

potential still dormant at best or worse still deliberately and seriously frustrated.[111]

3.8 The Synod of Bishops

The juridic nature of the Synod of Bishops is mainly found in *AS*, the *Ordi Synodi Episcoporum Celebrandae*[112] and in cc. 342–8 of *CIC*. There are no relevant references in *CIC/17* because there was no such forum. The Synod was created to meet a conciliar call for greater involvement by the episcopacy in universal church government. In 1959 Cardinal Bernardus Alfrink had advocated that a

> … permanent Council of specialised bishops, chosen from the church, could be given the charge of a legislative function in union with the Supreme Pontiff and the cardinals of the Roman Curia. The Roman Congregations would then maintain only a consultative and executive power.[113]

Also in 1959, Cardinal Silvio Oddi, suggested 'a permanent consultative body' which would 'meet periodically, even once a year, to discuss major concerns and to suggest possible new paths in the workings of the church'.[114] What they got was the Synod of Bishops, a non-legislative, non-standing, consultative body, convoked by the Pope at intervals of four years or so.

The manner of creation of the Synod of Bishops during Vatican II was strange. The Council fathers had agreed that the College of Bishops was the subject of full and supreme power over the universal church and were beginning to discuss ways of facilitating 'the participation of all the bishops in solicitude for the universal church'.[115] The pre-existing *schema* on bishops

---

111. See James A. Coriden, 'The Synod of Bishops: Episcopal Collegiality Still Seeks Adequate Expression', *The Jurist*, 64 (2004): 135.

112. See *AAS*, 59 (1967), 775–80, as revised in *AAS*, 61 (1969), 525–39 and *AAS*, 63 (1971), 702–4.

113. See Jan Grootaers, 'Une restauration de la theologie de l'episcopat.' Contribution du Cardinal Alfrink a la preparation de Vatican II. 'Glaube im process. Christsein nach dem 11 Vatikanum.' Fur Karl Rahner ed. Elmar Klinger, Klaus Wittstadt (Frieburg-Basel-Vienna 1984), 778–97.

114. See Motion tabled at Vatican II on 9.11.59 in *An Introduction to the Synod of Bishops*, Holy See Press Office, 1997. www.vatican.va/roman_curia/synod/index.html. [Accessed 10.10.2008.]

115. See *Acta Synodali Sacrosancti Concilii Oecuminici Vaticano II*, vol. III, 2:23–4, Indices, Vatican City, 1970.

and governance was revised to take account of their discussion. Beal et al. describe the revisions as 'gingerly worded'[116] but they provoked dissent. In a surprise move, Paul VI personally created the Synod of Bishops by *motu proprio*, *Apostolica sollicitudo* (*AS*)[117] while the Council was still sitting, making it a papal not a conciliar creation and raising the question whether his intervention 'anticipated or forestalled the achievement of a conciliar consensus'.[118]

The Synod was constructed as an advisory body to the Pope (c. 342), not engaged in decision making unless specifically requested by the Pope (c. 343). In the forty years and many Synods since, the Pope has never made such a request and Pope Benedict XVI is strongly against Synodal decision making on several grounds.

1. 'Such a Synod would simply amount to a second Curia.'[119]
2. 'Within the limited time of a synod – aside from special cases – deliberative powers cannot be exercised responsibly.'
3. Longer sessions 'are incompatible with the intrinsic nature of the episcopal ministry'.[120]
4. 'It is not an optional feature of the church's constitution to erect a second central power.'[121]

The notion that long sessions are incompatible with episcopal ministry could equally be extrapolated to Ecumenical Councils and confirms Beal et al.'s view mentioned above that there may now never be another Ecumenical Council. The reference to a second central power overlooks the fact that many commentators believed Vatican II to have recognised just such a second central power in the College of Bishops.

The Synod was to be a Rome based 'permanent Council of bishops for the universal church, to be directly and immediately subject to our power' (*AS*). It has never operated on a permanent

---

116.   Beal, Coriden and Green, eds, *New Commentary*, 454.
117.   See Pope Paul VI, Apostolic Letter *Apostolica Sollicitudo* (15 September 1965) in *AAS*, 57 (1965), 775–80.
118.   Beal, Coriden and Green, eds, *New Commentary*, 454.
119.   Joseph Ratzinger, *Church, Ecumenism and Politics: New Endeavours in Ecclesiology* (San Francisco: Ignatius Press, 2008), 57.
120.   Ibid., 58–9.
121.   Ibid., 59.

basis, meeting only periodically either in ordinary or extraordi-
nary form as well as in global or regional forms (c. 345).
Delegates are elected or chosen for a particular Synod only and
have no ongoing Synodal representational role between Synods.
Between 1967 and 2009 there were twelve Ordinary Plenary
Sessions, two Extraordinary and eight Special Synods. The first
Extraordinary General Assembly held in 1969 discussed episco-
pal collegiality and cooperation between the Pope and episcopal
conferences. Its most radical recommendations were that the
Synod meet every two years, that it's secretariat continue to
work between Synods and that the bishops be allowed to sug-
gest issues for the agenda. During the 1985 Special Synod,
Archeparch Hermaniuk, leader of Canada's Ukrainian Rite
Catholics, unsuccessfully requested the Synod to petition the
Pope for a permanent Synod that would act in the name of the
College of Bishops.[122] The 2001 Synod addressed the role of
Bishops but episcopal collegiality while much discussed, pro-
voked views as widely divergent as at Vatican II. Bishop Patrick
Dunn of New Zealand claimed that collegiality is 'the greatest
challenge for the church in our time' while Cardinal José Saraiva
Martins, believes, as mentioned before, that 'collegiality is by
now a very pacific theme, agreed upon by all, also in practice'.[123]

   Synods are convoked by the Pope, nowadays the time inter-
val stretching to four years. Advance preparations are laborious
with pre-synodal consultations involving patriarchates, bishops' conferences, heads of the Curial offices and the Union of
Superiors General, leading to a papally-approved agenda. The
Synod Council, assisted by experts, then drafts a *Lineamenta*
which on receipt of papal approval is distributed to all bishops
for local discussion. On receiving the results of those discussions the Synod Council prepares an *Instrumentum laboris*, also
subject to papal approval. It forms the basis for plenary discussion and has been sarcastically described as the outcome of the

122. See Richard Ortling, 'Frank Words from the Bishops', *Time* US, 21
     June 2005, www.time.com/magazine/article/09171,10784085-2,00.html.
     [Accessed 05.5.2009.]
123. See John L. Allen Jr, 'Collegiality vs. Centralization Dominates Synod,
     National Catholic Reporter, 12 October 2001, www.natcath.org/NCR_
     Online/archives2/2001d/101201/101201f.html. [Accessed 06.5.09.]

Synod, decided before it meets. The plenary sessions, which are held in camera are largely taken up with set piece formal statements on the *Instrumentum laboris* with very little time for interactive discussion, a matter, which along with the strong Curial involvement, has been criticised by Quinn.[124] Synodal reports are secret and go directly to the Pope who may issue a personal post-Synodal exhortation. In recent times some Synodal documents have been made public at the instigation of the Pope, indicating perhaps an evolution towards more openness. The Synodal section of the Vatican website says, 'So as to fulfill its mission, the Synod of Bishops works according to a methodology based on collegiality, a concept which characterises every stage of the Synod process from the first steps of preparation to the conclusions reached in each Synodal Assembly.'[125]

Neither the word 'college' nor 'collegial' appears in *AS* though the Vatican website says the Synod was designed 'to keep alive the spirit of collegiality engendered by the conciliar experience'.[126] Instead *AS* uses the word 'collaboration'. Pope Paul VI speaks of establishing 'even closer ties with the bishops in order to strengthen our union with those "whom the Holy Spirit has placed … to rule the church of God"' (Acts 20:28). This clearly acknowledges the bishops' divinely ordained power of universal governance yet the Synod is not a governance body. *CD* is relevant here. It says the Synod 'will be representative of the entire Catholic episcopate, it will reflect the participation of all the bishops in hierarchical communion in the care of the universal church' (*CD* Art 3). While the words 'representative' and 'participation' are highly ambiguous and the juridic relationship with the College of Bishops is not explained in either *AS* or *CD*, the Synod's representational role in relation to the College of Bishops acknowledged in both documents was deliberately omitted by the Code Revision Committee from c. 342 of *CIC* out

---

124. See John R. Quinn, *The Reform of the Papacy: The Costly Call to Christian Unity. Ut Unum Sint: Studies on Papal Primacy*, 110–16.

125. See Synod of Bishops, Synodal Information Chapter IV Notes on the Synodal process, www.vatican.va/roman_curia/synod/documents/rc_synod_20050309_documentation-profile_en.html. [Accessed 05.4.2009.]

126. Ibid., ch. 1.

of fears for its canonical consequences.[127] The argument goes that if the Synod is canonically representative of the College of Bishops it would be effectively a mini-Ecumenical Council with all the powers of such a council. In fact that need not be so. The larger body with full and supreme powers should be entitled to delegate to the smaller, representative body on terms as narrow or broad as it choses, if delegation is possible at all. However Pope Benedict XVI has said that in the event of any deliberative powers ever being conferred on the Synod they would 'inevitably ... be delegated papal authority, not authority proper to the Synod'.[128] What is not clear is whether any such papal delegation would be as Head of and on behalf of the College of Bishops.

Pope John Paul II was less cautious than Paul VI in using the word 'collegial' in speaking of the Synod of Bishops but equally evasive in dealing with the relationship between the Synod and the College of Bishops. Liberally using the word 'collegiality' he describes the Synod as,

> ... an instrument of collegiality whose 'dynamic force' ... is rooted in the proper understanding and life of the collegiality of the bishops. In fact the Synod is a particularly fruitful expression and the very valuable instrument of episcopal collegiality, that is, of the particular responsibility of the bishops around the Bishop of Rome.[129]

Lakeland says: 'Clearly, collegiality was important to John Paul. But what did he mean by collegiality?'[130] He answers that real collegiality in the Synod is a 'fiction' and its brand of 'collegiality' has developed into little more than curial centralisation,[131] a view strongly endorsed by Quinn:

> The Synod has not met the original expectations of its establishment and in reality the Curia sees itself as exercising oversight

---

127. See *Communicationes*, 14 (1982), 93.
128. Joseph Ratzinger, *Church, Ecumenism and Politics: New Endeavours in Ecclesiology*, 57.
129. Pope John Paul II, 'Discourse to the Council of the General Secretariat of the Synod of Bishops', 30 April 1983 in *AAS*, 75 (1983), 648–51 in *L'Osservatore Romano:* Weekly Edition in English, 23 May 1983, 5.
130. See Mannion, *The Vision of John Paul II: Assessing His Thought and Influence*, 184.
131. Ibid., 198.

and authority over the College of Bishops and worse still as subordinate to the Pope but superior to the College of Bishops.[132]

Pope John Paul II had a different outlook on the Synod, arguing that its pre-synodal consultations and plenary discussions
evidenced a truly universal 'exchange of information and suggestions'. He links its role directly to the College of Bishops saying that it is a

> way of expressing the collegiality of the bishops. The solidarity
> which binds them and the concern for the entire church are
> manifested to the highest degree when all the bishops are
> gathered *cum Petro et sub Petro* in the Ecumenical Council.
> Obviously, there exists a qualitative difference between the
> Council and the Synod, but notwithstanding that, the Synod
> expresses collegiality in a highly intense way, even while it does
> not equal that achieved by the Council.
>
> This collegiality is manifested principally in the collegial
> way the pastors of the local churches express themselves. When,
> especially after a good community preparation in their own
> churches and a collegial one in their episcopal conferences, with
> the responsibility of their own particular churches, but along
> with concern for the entire church, they together attest to the
> faith and the life of faith, their vote, if morally unanimous, has a
> qualitative ecclesial weight which surpasses the merely formal
> aspect of the consultative vote.[133]

In this one statement can be seen the elastic nature of the
word 'collegiality'. Pope John Paul applies several different
meanings to it in a relatively short address. The Synod he says
expresses conciliar episcopal collegiality by which he means affective not effective collegiality. Its views are weighty but only if
'morally unanimous', which sets a much higher bar than colleg -
iality implies elsewhere in the Code. The juridic relationship
between the Synod and the College of Bishops is conveniently
glossed over, just as it was in his homily at the conclusion of the
2001 Synod of Bishops where the Synod is described as being 'in
the name of the entire College of Bishops which we represent.'[134]

---

132. Quinn, 'The Claims of Primacy and the Costly Call to Unity', 116.
133. Pope John Paul II, 'Discourse to the Council of the General Secretariat of
      the Synod of Bishops.'
134. Homily of Pope John Paul II at the Conclusion of the Synod of Bishops, 27
      October 2001. English translation from Libreria Editrice Vaticana, www.vati-
      can.va/holy_father/john_paul_ii/homilies/2001/documents/hf_jp-
      ii_hom_20011027_closing-synod_en.html. [Accessed 01.4.2009.]

The facts do not support attaching any juridic significance to that statement. The Synod's *Instrumentum laboris* makes a similar claim in equally vague and juridically inaccurate terms:

> The College of Bishops cannot be conceived without communion with its visible head, the Roman Pontiff, a communion which is exercised in various forms of participation and collegiality … A specific form of collaboration with the Roman Pontiff is the Synod of Bishops, where a fruitful exchange of information and suggestions takes place, and, in light of the gospel and the teachings of the church, common trends of thought are formulated, which, once taken and proposed to all the church by the Successor of Peter, return to benefit the local churches.[135]

The verbal adroitness with which juridical problems are skimmed over or left to insinuation is notable but the reality is that while only members of the College of Bishops can be members of the Synod, the two have absolutely no formal juridic umbilical link. The Synod is a papal creation. It reports to the Pope not the College of Bishops nor does it report on behalf of the College.

Both Paul VI and John Paul II acknowledged the potential of the Synod to adapt and change. Paul VI stated 'This Synod … like all human institutions, can be improved upon with the passing of time' (*AS*), while Pope John Paul II has said, 'As every human institution, the Synod of Bishops also is growing and will be able to grow and to develop its potential even more, as moreover my predecessor foresaw in his Letter *Apostolica sollicitudo*.'[136] However Paul VI warned that the Synod is not a 'parliament'[137] and though Synodal discussions have been of profound influence throughout the universal church there is still a considerable difference between advising and legislating. Synodality is not power-sharing in the way that contemporary politics

---

135. Synod of Bishops, Ordinary General Assembly October 2001, *Instrumentum Laboris* 'Bishop: Servant of the Gospel of Jesus Christ for the Hope of the World', Art 69. English translation from Libreria Editrice Vaticana.

136. Pope John Paul II, 'Discourse to the Council of the General Secretariat of the Synod of Bishops.'

137. Pope Paul VI, Sunday Angelus, 22 September 1974, Synod of Bishops, Holy See Press Office, available www.vatican.va/news_services/press/documentazione/documents/sinodo_indice_en.ht. [Accessed 05.4.2009.]

might describe that phenomenon or as experienced in an Ecumenical Council. It is instead burden-sharing at a level considerably lower than decision taking. Lakeland criticises this failure to share legislative power as a bad example of 'affective collegiality, since its structure belies the trust that is supposed to reside in the affective bond'.[138] Quinn says the constant referral upwards to the Pope of such powers of governance as the bishops are permitted is a 'signal of distrust'.[139] Other voices disagree and powerfully. Avery Cardinal Dulles SJ writes that in general

> Quinn seems to present collegiality very much as though the College of Bishops were a kind of parliament, designed to offset the dangers of papal monarchy. According to the true theological conception, there is no conflict between primacy and collegiality. Each needs and serves the other. Nothing requires that the Pope, in exercising his primacy, be bound by the majority opinion of the bishops. He is obliged to exercise the special charisms of his office. If John XXIII had felt bound by the preponderant views of either his Curia or the world episcopate, Vatican II would probably not have been convened. But no reform of the papal office should undermine its capacity to safeguard the unity of the whole flock of Christ in the truth of revelation.[140]

Grötaers remarks of the 1969 and 1985 Synod of Bishops both of which discussed the role of the bishops, that though 'negative' in terms of collegial development they were nonetheless a 'unique experience of collegiality put into practice' for 'collegiality can be experienced partially and provisionally while waiting for its significance to be recognised fully and in ecclesial structures.'[141] This echoes Pope John Paul II's view that the Synod is a young institution in church terms with potential for development. The International Theological Commission says Synods can be a partial but true form of episcopal collegiality and that 'the collegial spirit will be able to promote the current forms of collegiality and invent new ones.'[142]

---

138.   Mannion, *The Vision of John Paul II: Assessing His Thought and Influence*, 198.
139.   See Quinn, 'The Claims of Primacy and the Costly Call to Unity', 116.
140.   Avery Cardinal Dulles SJ, 'Review of The Reform of the Papacy: The Costly Call to Christian Unity', by John R. Quinn. *First Things*, 104 (June/July 2000): 62–4.
141.   Jan Grotaers, 'Collegiality put to the Test', *Concilium*, 4 (1990): 28.
142.   See International Theological Commission. 'Select Themes of Ecclesiology' no. 6 in Michael Sharkey, ed., *International Theological Commission: Texts and Document* (San Francisco: Ignatius Press, 1987), 32–5.

These views present an optimistic, still-evolving future for collegiality. Others believe conciliar collegiality has delivered as much as it is ever going to. Coriden's scathing summary of the Synod of Bishops is that it is 'dysfunctional ... like so many children born and reared in the midst of conflict'.[143] He sees its existence as a betrayal of the Council, now 'merely nominal' and in need of considerable revision.[144] Such changes seem unlikely for the moment. The then Cardinal Ratzinger has argued that to make the Synod a deliberative body linked to the College of Bishops 'would further centralise the church, something most advocates of greater collegiality would oppose'.[145] He believes that instead of centralising power in this way there is a need to affirm 'the intrinsic bipolarity of the church's nature. This nature consists in the association of the full primatial authority ... with the living multiplicity of the local churches'.[146] He makes no mention of the governmental authority of the College of Bishops, presenting instead a constitutional view which on the face of it looks markedly pre-conciliar unless he has plans for greater two-way fluency between the centre and the circumference which are not yet known. For now, the living multiplicity of the local churches is a place with no way of explaining or describing itself fully and freely to the centre.

3.9 The College of Cardinals
The College of Cardinals is the only episcopal body which is reasonably regularly involved in effective episcopal collegial governance insofar as it elects Popes and governs the church on a care and maintenance basis during a Vacant See. This clear-cut collegial role long predates Vatican II, owes nothing to conciliar collegiality and cannot have been absent from the Council fathers minds in discussing collegiality. Placed between the Synod of Bishops and the Curia in *CIC*, the College of Cardinals is described as a 'special college' (c. 349). It is governed by customised special laws most of which do not appear in the Code

143. James A. Coriden, 'The Synod of Bishops: Episcopal Collegiality Still Seeks Adequate Expression', 116.

144. Ibid., 135.

145. Joseph Ratzinger, *Church, Ecumenism and Politics: New Endeavours in Ecclesiology*, 57.

146. Ibid.

but are to be found in a variety of papal documents.[147] While
under the direct authority of the Pope, it is presided over by a
dean (c. 352) who is first among equals (c. 352 §1) though voting
and office-holding rights among members are age-differentiat-
ed. The College of Cardinals is a collegial juridic person within the terms of c. 115 §2, an ecclesial construct with such powers as ecclesial rather than divine law accords to it and amenable
to the rules governing such juridic persons (cc. 113–23). It is the
only college at episcopal level which comes close to the description in the *Nota*.

The college's best known and most dramatic role is that of
papal elector, for the College of Cardinals alone elects the Pope
(c. 349). The College also 'governs' the universal church (on a
caretaker basis), during any interregnum subject to cc. 335, 359,
428 §1 and the Apostolic Constitution *Universi Dominici gregis*. It
does not take the place of the Pope nor does it have his legislative powers in respect of the church (it has slightly wider emer-
gency powers of civil governance of the Vatican State). It cannot
take decisions (apart from the choosing of a new Pope) which
would bind a future Pope.

CIC/17 had 'limited the collegial exercise of the papal office
both actually and legally to cooperation between the Pope and
the College of Cardinals … Vatican II … broadened the circle of
those able to participate in this collegiality'.[148] Canon 334 gives
effect to this, in particular placing the bishops at the top of the
list of those who may assist the Pope. In aiding the Pope the
Cardinals are said to act either collegially when they 'are summoned together' (in ordinary or extraordinary consistories c. 353)
or the Council of Cardinals[149] or 'individually' for example
through the Curial offices they hold (c. 349). Generally ordinary
consistories involve only the Cardinals who are based in Rome
(c. 353 §2). The less frequent extraordinary consistories require

---

147.   For more relevant recent Papal norms see Paul VI, *motu proprio, Sacro
       Cardinalis Consilio*, 26 February 1965 in *AAS*, 57 (1965), 296–7: *Motu proprio,
       Ingravescentem Aetatem*, 21 November 1970 in *AAS*, 62 (1970), 811 and
       Apostolic Constitution *Romano Pontifico Eligendo*, 1 October 1975 in *AAS*
       67 (1975), 605–45: see also Pope John Paul II, Apostolic Constitution
       Universi Dominici Gregis, 22 February 1996 in *AAS*, 88 (1996), 305–43.
148.   See Beal, Coriden and Green, eds, *New Commentary*, 442.
149.   The Council of Cardinals for the Study of Organisational and Economic
       Questions of the Apostolic See is made up of fifteen cardinals appointed
       by the Pope for a five-year term of office.

all the Cardinals to be called together (c. 353 §3). They are advisory, not decision making bodies (outside the matter of selecting
a Pope). As individuals working in the Curia, Cardinals have
been described as assisting 'the Supreme Pontiff in governing
the universal church' (*PB* Introd. 9), a description which should
be as juridically meaningless as saying that any secular Civil
Service assists a Prime Minister to govern, but in church structures the line between legislative and executive functions are so
poorly differentiated that the claim could well be *de facto* true
but legally suspect.

Molano describes the collaboration between the Pope and
Synod of Bishops, the Cardinals and other advisers, as 'a manifestation of a certain collegiality' though he advises that 'it will
not always be easy to distinguish between personal exercise and
collegial exercise of governance'.[150] This observation is particul -
arly true in the case of the College of Cardinals for when invited
by the Pope to assist him, the College of Cardinals acts collegially
if they advise him as a group and non-collegially if they assist
him as individuals (c. 349). In both cases the Pope himself acts
collegially in the broad sense but juridically speaking he may be
acting either collegially or personally!

CIC makes no mention of the relationship, juridic or otherwise,
between the College of Bishops and the College of Cardinals or
between the College of Cardinals and the Synod of Bishops.
Paul VI alluded to a plan to add the members of the Synodal
Council to the papal electorate[151] but it came to nothing. None of
these bodies have been identifiably juridically plugged into one
another or clearly distinguished from one another in terms of
their roles. Historically the College of Cardinals was an influential discussion chamber with the Pope which over time became
largely ceremonial. Beal et al. point out that in more recent times
'John Paul II has increasingly consulted the College of Cardinals
on diverse matters of universal church governance'[152] but it is
'not entirely clear' why he might consult the Synod on some
things and the College of Cardinals on others.[153]

---

150.   *Exegetical Commentary*, vol. II/1, 587.
151.   See Pope Paul VI, Allocution to the Council of the General Secretariat of
       the Synod of Bishops, 24 March 1973.
152.   See Beal, Coriden and Green, eds, *New Commentary*, 471.
153.   Ibid.

In the past not all Cardinals were bishops or even holders of sacred orders but since 1962 by *motu proprio, Cum gravissima*[154] all Cardinals are supposed to be bishops and so members of the College of Bishops (though there remains still a small number of Cardinals who are not bishops). It is this relatively recent alignment of the membership of both bodies which raises serious issues about the juridic relationship between the College of Cardinals and the College of Bishops. Although Beal et al. say that 'according to current opinion, the College of Cardinals is representative of the College of Bishops,'[155] there must be substantial doubts about the juridic base of any such representative role. Such questions were not discussed at Vatican II, nor have there been clear directives on the matter since. The overlap of membership between the groupings is obvious but what is not obvious is the legal/constitutional nature of the link. The Synod of Bishops and the College of Cardinals are mandated to report directly to the Pope, not to or through the College of Bishops. They are 'optional' ecclesial constructs which the Pope could abolish. He cannot do the same to the College of Bishops for it is a divine construct like the papacy though historically some canonists have argued that the College of Cardinals succeeded to the Apostolic College. Beal et al. say most canonists insisted that the College's 'rights derived from the Pope even when the Roman See was vacant'.[156]

Yet the College of Cardinals is important to the debate on episcopal collegiality for here is one group of bishops which does have specific decision making powers and special, albeit restricted, powers of governance. These owe nothing to Vatican II and remain unaffected so far by its recognition of the divinely ordained, full and supreme power of governance of the College of Bishops. The collegial protocols set out in the General Norms are very evidently at work in the College of Cardinals in ways that are absent from the College of Bishops and the Synod of Bishops.

---

154. See Pope John XXIII, *motu proprio, Cum gravissima*, 15 April 1962 in *AAS*, 54 (1962), 256–8.

155. See Beal, Coriden and Green, eds, *New Commentary*, 449.

156. Ibid., 465.

As an institution the College of Cardinals has a long history. The membership, powers and responsibilities have all been dramatically altered since the eighth century both by ecumenical councils (though not Vatican II) and by Popes, the latter authoring most of the changes. They could be altered again to give the College of Cardinals a more cogent juridic relationship to the College of Bishops though Pope Benedict XVI's constitutional objections (mentioned above) to making a second central authority of the Synod are every bit as applicable to the College of Cardinals. The canonical problems of creating a pleni-potent mini-Ecumenical Council which worried the Code commission in relation to the Synod of Bishops would also apply here but they could equally easily be dealt with by clear mandate of delegation, as limited or wide as the mandate permits. In fact the College of Cardinals has long operated with such delegated limited mandates from the Pope without any major difficulty.

For now though the College of Cardinals is just another part of the ill-fitting jigsaw puzzle which is church governance and episcopal collegiality. When operating as a college engaged in specific deliberative matters concerning governance of the universal church during an interregnum, the cardinals are the surest and most regular manifestation of effective collegiality, for they have a clear juridic platform and a direct, albeit limited role in universal church governance. As such their role and that of Ecumenical Councils are the only fully realised practical examples of effective i.e. fully juridic collegiality. Both pre-date Vatican II and as the only then (and now) extant examples of effective episcopal collegiality, must be regarded as models of practice which were exemplars of episcopal collegiality when it was discussed by the Council Fathers. Yet forty years after Vatican II, effective juridic episcopal collegiality begins and ends with these two non-Vatican II constructs. The additional Vatican II provision for extra-conciliar collegial action by the College of Bishops remains unused. Beyond these the word 'collegial' embraces forms of church collaboration and consultation which, important though they are, lack similar juridic effect but not juridic confusion.

3.10 The Roman Curia

The *Instrumentum laboris* of the 2001 Synod of Bishops says that in communion

> ... with the Roman Pontiff, all bishops are members of the Episcopal College ... A fruit and expression of this collegial union is the collaboration of bishops from every part of the globe in the offices of the Holy See, particularly in the Departments of the Roman Curia (Art 69).

The Curia is the Rome-based 'civil service' of the universal church, defined as 'the complex of dicasteries and institutes which help the Roman Pontiff in the exercise of his supreme pastoral office for the good and service of the whole church and of the particular churches' (*PB* Introd. 1). It is intimately involved in the universal church's day to day administration, with selected Cardinals generally heading up its many and diverse offices. Its staff are mainly clerics with the reasonably recent addition of a smattering of laity. Between the Curia and the College of Cardinals there is an identifiable link for it was the sixteenth-century division of the latter into separate dicasteries (also described as 'colleges' in *PB* Introd. 4) which created the formal structure from which the Curia evolved. Much of the law governing it is to be found outside of *CIC* in special laws, notably *Pastor Bonus*, the most recent attempt at updating the Curia, a labyrinthine body of indeterminate powers, which has grown unevenly over many centuries.

The Curia came in for unflattering comment at Vatican II as it had at Vatican I. Just as in the secular world people are apt to criticise the anonymous mandarins in Brussels, or the faceless bureaucrats in a government department so too the centralised, Rome-based Curia, has come in for its share of similar reproach. *CD* acknowledged the need for Curial reform, through modern - ising its structure, making its staff more representative of the universal church, and allowing for greater involvement of lay people (*CD* 9–10).

Looking first at the very brief provisions in *CIC* there is no mention of 'college' or 'collegiality' in either of the two relevant canons. The Curia itself is not a college (*PB* Introd. 10). More importantly there is no mention of the College of Bishops. The Curia operates in the name of the Pope and by his authority

(c. 360). *CD* says the Pope 'employs the various departments of the Roman Curia' (*CD* 9). Beal et al. say that

> ... while the Curia is evidently closely linked to the Pope, it should also be viewed ideally as linked to all the bishops. Its being composed significantly of cardinals and bishops bespeaks a certain 'collegial' character although not in the proper sense of the term.[157]

This raises a query about the relationship between the Curia and the College of Bishops, one that is neither addressed in *CIC*, nor clarified in *PB*. Juridically there is none in the sense that the Curia does not act in the name of nor does it report to the College of Bishops. It serves the Head of the College and reports to him but nowhere is that reporting relationship expressed in those terms. *PB* to the extent that it addresses that relationship at all paints a distinctly primatial picture. There Pope John Paul II speaks of Christ entrusting his divine mission to the bishops and 'in a singular way' to the Pope. In addressing the hierarchical nature of the church and the service of *communio* by both Pope and bishops, he describes the bishops as being 'holders of office in government' (*PB* Introd. 2). This is actually true only of the Pope himself. The bishops and cardinals who work within the Curia and who hold various important offices should no more be said to be holders of office in government than any senior civil servant in a secular state. They work for the government but they themselves are not 'in government'. In fact this phrase of Pope John Paul II's goes to the very heart of the matter. The College of Bishops is a holder of power and authority over the universal church but apart from its Head, no single other member holds an office 'in government', through which he exercises the divinely instituted power of the College of Bishops. When the Pope meets his Curial colleagues, even at the level of Secretary of State, he meets them in exercise of his divine authority. They meet him as subordinate support staff, in exercise of authority delegated to them by the Pope. Pope John Paul II puts it thus in this extract from the Introduction to *PB*:

> Our predecessor Sixtus V, in the Apostolic Constitution *Immensa æterni Dei*, admitted as much: 'The Roman Pontiff, whom Christ

---

157.   Ibid., 477.

the Lord constituted as visible head of his body, the church, and appointed for the care of all the churches, calls and rallies unto himself many collaborators for this immense responsibility ... so that he, the holder of the key of all this power, may share the huge mass of business and responsibilities among them – i.e. the cardinals – and the other authorities of the Roman Curia, and by God's helping grace avoid breaking under the strain' (*PB* Introd. 3).

It is fascinating to see how Pope John Paul attempts to reconcile this pre-Vatican II description with his claim that in *PB* he wanted to ensure that 'the structure and working methods of the Roman Curia increasingly correspond to the ecclesiology spelled (*sic*) out by the Second Vatican Council' (*PB* Introd. 13). One might have expected that ecclesiology to involve in some way the governance role of the College of Bishops. Yet in *PB* this is one area that is glaringly downplayed despite much discussion and many descriptions of the episcopal college's role; the college endures in the same way that the papacy is permanent; it is intimately linked to the Petrine office (*PB* Introd. 8); it shepherds the church without interruption; it expresses the multifariousness and universality of the church; its power is that of a servant (*PB* Introd. 2); the visible sign of its interdependence with the Pope is the Curia (*PB* Introd. 3); the Curial counsels to the Pope are collegial (*PB* Introd. 4); the Curia does not block communion between the College of Bishops and the Pope, to the contrary it facilitates it (*PB* Introd. 8); the composition of the Curia proves how closely bound it is to the bishops of the whole world (*PB* Introd. 9); the collegial spirit between the bishops and their head works through the Roman Curia (*PB* Introd. 9–10); the Curia, bishops, Pope and people form one body characterised by unity of faith and unity of discipline (*PB* Introd. 11).

When distilled, despite judicious employment of the term 'collegial' *PB* exudes a strong sense of primatialism, with *communio*, unity and service the updated language for describing the subsidiary and subordinate role played at universal governance level by the episcopal college. The college's role though divinely instituted is exercised through a Curia which is not a divinely instituted body, exists at the will of the Pope and exercises jurisdiction only by way of delegation from him and for him. *PB* reflects Pope John Paul II's own strong centralising tendencies which, according to Lakeland, he saw as a bulwark against the kind of abuses he had witnessed in his native Poland.[158] How has this impacted on the episcopal collegiality envisaged by Vatican II? Lash minces no words:

> Perhaps the greatest failure of the conciliar programme of reform has ... been ecclesial or ecclesiological. Nobody, I think foresaw the possibility that, 50 years later, the offices of the Roman Curia should have increased their control over the church. Not only does the coagulation of power at the centre frustrate the ability of the episcopate to recover a proper sense of episcopal authority and the development of appropriate structures of collegial governance, but it has weakened the recognition of the indispensability of the *sensus fidelium*.[159]

Cardinal König comes close to saying that the Curia has virtually usurped the governance role appropriate to the College of Bishops.

> Paul VI took pains to remodel the advisory and controlling function of the curial authorities, in order to bring them into line with the council's intentions. In the post-conciliar period, however, as bishops have not infrequently pointed out, the Vatican authorities have striven to take back autonomy and central leadership for themselves. The intentions of *Sollicitudo omnium ecclesiarum* have not been realised ... the Roman Curia remains a powerful force tending in the opposite direction, towards centralism ... *de facto* and not *de jure*, intentionally or unintentionally, the Curia authorities working in conjunction with the Pope have appropriated the tasks of the episcopal college. It is they who now carry out almost all of them.[160]

Quinn develops much the same point.

> The Curia is the arm of the Pope. But the Curia always runs the real risk of seeing itself as a *tertium quid*. When this happens, in place of the dogmatic structure comprised of the Pope and the rest of the episcopate, there emerges a new and threefold structure: The Pope, the Curia and the episcopate. This makes it possible for the Curia to see itself as exercising oversight and authority over the College of Bishops, to see itself as subordinate to the Pope but superior to the College of Bishops. To the

---

158. Mannion, *The Vision of John Paul II: Assessing His Thought and Influence*, 199.
159. Nicholas Lash, 'Could the Shutters yet Come Down?', 13.
160. Cardinal König, 'My Vision for the Church of the Future', *The Tablet*, 27 March 1999: 4.

degree that this is so and is reflected in the policies and actions of the Curia it obscures and diminishes both the doctrine and the reality of episcopal collegiality.[161]

These comments suggest that while the Curia is technically at best a manifestation of affective collegiality, it acts as if it was ersatz effective collegiality. That this should be so is probably not so surprising. Even one-man primatialism needs many hands to do its work and the culture of strict primatial authority articulated at Vatican I had a considerable head start over the new concept of conciliar episcopal collegiality, left hanging, ambiguous and uncoordinated after Vatican II. The Curia of the twentieth century was a child of centuries of primatialism, with a direct lineage, not to the College of Bishops but to the College of Cardinals and a direct reporting relationship to the Pope which was left undisturbed by the Council. Its juridic relationship to the College of Bishops both before and after *CIC* and *PB* is moot. Unlike the College of Bishops, the Curia's offices, roles, powers and structures are highly developed and organisationally strong. It has its place in the daily scheme of things in ways that the College of Bishops does not. Post Vatican II Curial staff are more representative of the universal episcopacy and marginally more representative of the laity but the Curia's contribution to conciliar collegiality is wide open for debate.

3.11 Ad Limina Apostolorum *Visits*

Despite the efforts of some writers to restrict the idea of colleg-iality to discussions of church governance at the universal gov-ernance level, the word 'collegial' is liberally used in relevant church documents when discussing the work of bishops at local or regional level. *PB* uses it several times when describing *ad limina apostolorum* (*ad limina*) visits. *CIC/17* c. 340 provided for such visits so they are not a creation of conciliar collegiality. The visits are made quinquennially by diocesan bishops and involve a pilgrimage to the tombs of Sts Peter and Paul, submission of a pro forma diocesan report, a brief meeting with the Pope and discussions with Curia personnel. The *Instrumentum laboris* of the 2001 Synod says *ad limina* visits are 'An important manifestation

---

161.   Quinn, 'The Claims of Primacy and the Costly Call to Unity.'

of communion with the Pope and the offices of the Holy See' (Art 70). Such visits are governed by detailed provisions in special law as well as two canons (cc. 399 and 400) in *CIC* neither of which makes reference to the word 'collegial'.

Ad limina visits are said to foster communion and unity 'to the highest degree' (*PB* 29) and to serve the values of catholicity and collegiality (*PB* Appendix 1, 4). *Ad limina* visits are specific - ally related to the individual bishop's *munera* of teaching, sancti- fying and governing his particular diocese but *PB* connects them explicitly to the universal mission of the College of Bishops. Although diocesan bishops do not exert their diocesan authority by way of delegated mandate from the College of Bishops, the following paragraph seems to visualise them collectively as expressing locally the universal *munera* of the college.

> *Ad limina* visits express that pastoral solicitude which thrives in the universal church. Here we see the meeting of the pastors of the church, joined together in a collegial unity that is based on apostolic succession. In this college, each and every one of the bishops displays that solicitude of Jesus Christ, the Good Shepherd, which all have received by way of inheritance (*PB* Appendix 1, 4).

This connection seems not to have any visible juridic implic - ations but to be related to what Gomez-Iglesias calls the 'ancient and venerable theological and canonical roots'[162] of the tradition of *ad limina* visits, which over generations reinforced the global centrality and source of unity that is the See of Rome. Leaving aside the imposition on the Pope's time, the brevity of individ- ual contact, the formulaic nature of the information shared and the contemporary drift towards considerable backlog, there are visible gaps in such a minimalist, non-probative system of epis- copal accountability albeit that the Curia routinely responds to the bishops' reports with comments, guidance and suggestions. The acknowledged level of systemic failure within diverse geo- graphic areas of the church with regard to child protection in particular, raises suspicions that *ad limina* visits had become set pieces which failed to get to grips with sensitive issues. Had pre- 1990s *ad limina* visits been doing their job properly, the Pope and

---

162. *Exegetical Commentary*, vol. II/1, 840.

the Curia should have been the best informed group in the world about the extent and nature of the problem of clerical sex abuse and well placed to act on the matter long before local episcopacies were forced to take action in response to public pressure or civil investigations. The civil authorities' Commission of Investigation's Report into the Catholic Archdiocese of Dublin of July 2009 says that according to the Archbishop of Dublin Dr Diarmuid Martin the first reference he could find to clerical child abuse in a diocesan *ad limina* report was in 1999.[163] 'It was a very simple statement that the archdiocese had gone through a difficult time, that there had been allegations of child sexual abuse and that priests had been convicted.' The Commission remarked that notifying the Congregation for the Doctrine of the Faith of such cases 'was not the practice of previous archbishops though it appears to have been a mandatory requirement of Canon Law at least since 1917'.[164] If it were ever to transpire such information had indeed been long in the possession of the Curia it could be to quote Lord Denning in another context 'an appalling vista'[165] with serious implications for authority in the church.

Ad limina reports, travel upwards to the Pope and the Curia but there is neither a requirement nor a practice that they are published to the diocesan faithful. Reportage generally takes the form today of a website photograph of the bishop with the Pope and a few innocuous anecdotal lines about the visit. If *ad limina* visits contribute at all to a generalised affective collegiality it is at the immediate level of reinforcement of episcopal solidarity with and obeisance to the Pope, as well as practical help and encouragement to the individual bishop from the centre.

3.12 Episcopal Councils and Conferences
Leisching says that 'episcopal collegiality is at work in any action in which the concern of bishops for other particular churches

---

163. Commission of Investigation: Report into the Catholic Archdiocese of Dublin, 53 (Dublin: Dept of Justice, Equality and Law Reform, July 2009), www.justice.ie/en/JELR/Pages/PB09000504. [accessed 14.03.2010.]
164. Ibid.
165. See McIlkenny-v-Chief Constable of the West Midlands [1980] Q.B. 283 at 323D.

than those entrusted to them is expressed'.[166] The *Instrumentum laboris* of the 2001 Synod of Bishops twins this collegiality with 'communion'.

> Bishops live their communion with other bishops in the exercise of episcopal collegiality. Since Christian antiquity, this reality of communion has been particularly expressed in the celebration of ecumenical councils and particular councils, both plenary and provincial. Even today, such councils maintain their usefulness as seen in the current institution of Episcopal Conferences' (Art 71).

Although diocesan bishops exert a personal authority over their own diocese which is jealously guarded by Canon Law and instituted by divine will, not papal delegation, groupings or gathering of bishops have been a feature of the church from its earliest times. Some members of such groupings may be Archbishops, Metropolitans, Cardinals or Conference Presidents but these titles confer virtually no hierarchical control by one bishop over another. Episcopal groupings occur at all levels of the church from the College of Bishops (which meets at universal church level currently once a century), to those which meet at local, national, regional and international level, such as ecclesiastical provinces of neighbouring dioceses (c. 431) or ecclesiastical regions (c. 433), plenary councils (c. 439), provincial councils (c. 440) and Episcopal Conferences (c. 447) including their transnational and supranational forms.

Particular Councils though cumbersome not only had a long historical pedigree but importantly had, and still have, valuable legislative powers (c. 455).Though they do not legislate for the universal church, they are arguably a long-standing pre-conciliar form of juridic effective collegiality operating at national level. They have however waned in usage, though *CD* (as Vatican I had also done) expressed the hope that they would be used more regularly. In fact they have been overtaken nowadays by the less formal, more frequent, and juridically less powerful Episcopal Conferences. Tanner argues that by letting the practice of holding councils fall into disuse, the church has found it difficult to come to terms adequately with major shifts

---

166.   Peter Leisching, 'Conferences of Bishops' in Provost and Walf, *Collegiality Put to the Test*, 83.

and fault-lines over the course of modern history, from the Enlightenment to contemporary so-called relativism. He favours increased conciliarism throughout the church by holding smaller councils (with legislative powers) outside of Europe rather than a Vatican III, which he argues is not called for since Vatican II is still in the process of being worked through.[167] Such bodies would have greater time for preparation and reflection than Episcopal Conferences which are often in the immediate eye of politico-social issues though such conferences have a flexibility, accessibility and immediacy which have helped local churches muster timely (whatever about effective) collective responses to contemporary, thorny issues.

From the mid-nineteenth century informal gatherings of bishops in certain countries began to develop to deal with local and regional pastoral issues which benefited from a collaborative cross-diocesan approach. By Vatican II there were over forty such groups. Their popularity was growing but they were outside of any canonical system. They were gathered into the ecclesial mainstream by *CD* 38 and brought under more evident official control by *motu proprio* of Paul VI *Ecclesiae Sanctae*.[168] *LG* saw them as 'in a position to contribute in many and fruitful ways to the concrete realisation of the collegial spirit' (*LG* 23). At the time of the Council, Ratzinger had a positive view of them (later to change) as a part-realisation of collegiality.[169] Canons 447–59 of *CIC* now govern their operation. Their theological status is disputed, though Leisching claims that 'the theological basis for them lies in the collegiality of the episcopate, which in turn has its foundation in the church as *communio*'.[170] In response to queries over their theological and canonical status Pope John Paul II issued the *motu proprio, Apostolos Suos*,[171] probably the most important post-Conciliar papal document on

167. See Norman Tanner, *Was the Church Too Democratic? Councils, Collegiality and the Church's Future*.

168. See Paul VI, Apostolic Letter Ecclesiae Sanctae, 6 August 1966 in *AAS* 58 (1966), 757–87.

169. See Joseph Ratzinger, *Das Neue Volk Gottes. Entwürfe Zur Ekklesiologie* (Dusseldorf: Patmos, 1969), 222.

170. Peter Leisching, 'Conferences of Bishops' in Provost and Walf, *Collegiality put to the Test*, 79.

171. John Paul II, Apostolic Letter *Apostolos Suos*.

episcopal collegiality generally though it was designed to deal with the theological and juridical nature of episcopal conferences.

ApS acknowledges that the apostles 'constituted an undivided body' (*ApS* 1) and that the 'Bishops have by divine institution taken the place of the apostles' (*ApS* 2). It speaks of the 'collegial spirit which inspired the establishment of episcopal conferences and guides their activity' (*ApS* 5) and their role in 'strengthening ecclesial communion' (*ApS* 6). But this spirit of collegiality is not to be confused with the effective juridic collegiality of the College of Bishops.

> Equivalent collegial actions cannot be carried out at the level of individual particular churches or of gatherings of such churches called together by their respective bishops. At the level of particular churches grouped together by geographic areas (by countries, regions, etc.), the bishops in charge do not exercise pastoral care jointly with collegial acts equal to those of the College of Bishops' (*ApS* Art 10).

This means that Episcopal Conferences are a 'concrete application of collegial spirit (*affectus collegialis*)' (*ApS* 12) but they never take on 'the collegial nature proper to the actions of the order of bishops as such, which alone holds the supreme power over the whole church [and] which as a theological subject is indivisible' (*ApS* 12). Pope John Paul II's words could not be more emphatic, 'episcopal collegiality in the strict and proper sense belongs only to the entire College of Bishops' (*ApS* Art 12).

ApS purports to settle the juridic status of Episcopal Conferences which the Vatican Council Commission and the Council fathers had been unable to resolve. It follows closely Ghirlanda's argument that the Episcopal Conference is only loosely collegial in the sense of affective collegiality and is no more than a pragmatic construct of convenience, which cannot transcend the divinely instituted autonomy of each bishop and so has no group entitlement to the *obsequium* of the faithful.[172] *ApS* falls some way short of Örsy's view of Episcopal Conferences as linear descendants of the regional councils or particular Synods of the early church, and as essential elements of conciliar *communio* and collegiality, which can in his view be exercised in

---

172.   See Gianfranco Ghirlanda, 'De Episcoporum Conferentia Deque Exercitio Potestatis Magisterii', 573–603.

different degrees, the greater being ecumenical councils and lesser being other groupings of bishops.[173]

In *CIC*, Episcopal Conferences are dealt with outside of the chapter on the hierarchical constitution of the church which adds validity to the clarifications of *ApS*. Although some, like Hamer, argued at the Council for an indivisible episcopal collegiality that would manifest itself at both universal and local level[174] and Green sees episcopal conferences as an 'obligatory institutionalisation of the collegial responsibility of the bishops for the welfare of the church and the larger society',[175] there is a juridic line in the sand here. That said, the growth of Episcopal Conferences from the second half of the twentieth century undoubtedly owes much to the conciliar spirit of collegiality and to *CD*'s exhortation in support of the development of both episcopal conferences and subsidiarity. It also owes a lot to the assertiveness of clusters of regional bishops and general papal tolerance. The number of these now mandatory conferences has grown to well over one hundred and there has been a marked increase in the development of trans and supranational conferences. Though they have no lay membership, all such conferences are often deeply exposed to and involved in contemporary ecclesial and civic debates and they draw in wide-ranging advice and expertise from outside the episcopacy. In this way as Duffy says the bishops not only hold 'a vertical consensus in teaching with the past' but attempt 'to find and express a horizontal consensus with the living faith ... of the church at large'.[176] With communications along the vertical and horizontal lines so stage-managed and circumscribed this assertion may only be fully true of the bishops talking among themselves.

LG 23 and *CD* 38 were anxious to bring Episcopal Conferences under more effective papal control and the control of Canon

---

173. See Ladislas Örsy, 'The Teaching Authority of Episcopal Conferences' in Thomas J. Reese, ed., *Episcopal Conferences: Historical, Canonical and Theological Studies*, 233–52.

174. See Jerome Hamer, 'Les Conférence Épiscopales, Exércise De La Collégialité', *Nouvelle Théologique*, 85 (1963): 966–9.

175. See Thomas Green, 'Normative Role of Episcopal Conferences in the 1983 Code' in Thomas J. Reese, ed., *Episcopal Conferences: Historical, Canonical and Theological Studies*, 142.

176. See Eugene Duffy, 'Episcopal Conferences in the Context of Communion: Some Notes on the American Experience', *The Jurist*, 64 (2004): 167.

Law. They were made compulsory and given added impetus and status on the one hand but they were also taken in hand on the other. They were recognised as having the right in certain limited circumstances (where universal law or special papal mandate allows) to pass binding decrees (which are subject to papal approval) by a two-thirds majority decision (*CD* 37–8 and c. 455). Outside of such specifically mandated areas of legislative competence Episcopal Conferences cannot bind individual bishops and so even while developing greater collaborative structures, they struggle with the discipline of collegiality among themselves. In Ireland for example, National Guidelines on the reporting of clerical sex abuse cases, promulgated by the Episcopal Conference were secretly derogated from by some individual bishops without the knowledge of their fellow bishops or of the public. The Statutes of the Bishops' Conference of England and Wales provide for notification to the President of the Conference of any such individual derogation from conference resolutions which do not have juridic force but which are expected to be observed 'by all members in the spirit of collegial unity'.[177] De Quieroga, writing of the Brazilian Bishops Conference, claims that it 'has a genuinely collegial way of working, which makes it difficult for unilateral or arbitrary decisions to be taken, or for any body or post to operate in isolation'.[178] The existence of Episcopal Conferences has made them, rather than Rome or individual bishops, the locus of management of public controversies concerning the church and usually under intense media scrutiny. Some of the encounters have been bruising and the controversies very damaging to local churches but the existence of conferences, with their ability to meet speedily and informally has been essential to maintaining ecclesial equilibrium and credibility.

Episcopal Conferences were not specifically designed to be legislative bodies unlike particular councils which do have 'power of governance, especially legislative power' (c. 445) and the majority voting thresholds in Episcopal Conferences are

---

177. See Statutes of the Catholic Bishops' Conference of England and Wales, June 1987, Art 16.

178. Gervásio Fernandes de Quieroga, 'The Brazilian Experience' in Provost and Walf, *Collegiality put to the Test*, 117.

much stricter than in particular councils. Canon 447 establishes
the Episcopal Conference as a permanent assembly (which particular and provincial councils are not) of bishops of a country or
territory. There then follow ten formal and relatively straightforward canons devoted to the legal underpinnings of such conferences, such as creation and suppression, juridical status,
statutes, structure, membership, meetings, voting rights, legislative competency, recording of business etc. The final canon in
the section, c. 459, is almost casual by comparison for it simply
rehearses what had been stated in *CD* that relations are to be fos-
tered between Episcopal Conferences, especially neighbouring
ones. Yet out of what Wiljens describes as this 'passing'[179] reference there has developed a host of fresh inter-conference initiatives such as the Council of European Bishops' Conferences
(CCEE), the Commission of the Bishops' Conferences of the
European Community (COMECE), the Latin American
Episcopal Council (CELAM), the Symposium of Episcopal
Conferences of Africa and Madagascar (SECAM) and the
Federation of Asian Bishops' Conferences (FABC). Like CELAN
(Conference of Bishops of Latin America) which had existed
since 1955, the idea and demand for these new structures did
not grow from the centre out but from the periphery in. Quinn
instances the Second European Ecumenical Assembly in Graz in
1997 as an example of the growing momentum of episcopal conferences for it was organised in cooperation between COMECE
and the bodies representing other Christian denominations
without any official participation by the Curia or the Pope.[180]
These bodies have a visible dynamic which has helped the
church maintain a place of relevance and engagement in the
civic and secular governmental space, e.g. in dealing with the
institutions of the European Union. Without them, that space
might well have disappeared. However it must be remembered,
as the *Instrumentum laboris* of the 2001 Synod points out, that
these international and supranational Episcopal Conferences
while useful instruments of informal collaboration, do not
have the competence of 'properly called Episcopal Conferences

---

179. Mariam Wijlens, 'Structures for Episcopal Leadership for Europe', *The
      Jurist*, 61 (2001): 192.
180. See Quinn, 'The Claims of Primacy and the Costly Call to Unity.'

according to the norms of canon law' (Art 72). In other words they lack juridic status. These are however relatively young institutions in church terms and as de Fleurquin says 'call for much patience and the time which is needed for maturity and growth'.[181]

The development of Episcopal Conferences has produced a formidable array of critics with de Lubac[182] and Ratzinger expressing serious concerns[183] about their drift towards nationalism and away from universal unity, their capacity to erode the individual responsibility (and courage) of bishops and their creation of fora where the weakness of the lowest denominator would prevail. Others see such caution as undisguised primatialism and centralism, the voices of those 'afraid of no longer being masters in their own houses.[184]

3.13 Diocesan Synods

The diocesan synod is probably the last stop on the most extenuated affective episcopal collegiality line, though in truth there is a marked reluctance by even the most ardent supporters of such Synods to describe them in terms of ecclesial never to mind episcopal collegiality. They are not so described in *CIC*. Cusack, a lay diocesan chancellor, in writing of the role and potential of the diocesan synod never once alludes to it as a collegial forum or a vehicle for the expression of collegiality within the church.[185] It is evident too in the writing of Wijlens that collegiality applies only to interaction between bishops themselves, including the Pope. Every other form of participative interaction is something else, though she acknowledges, along with Legrand, that the council paid insufficient attention to collegiality in the context of a bishop and his local church.[186]

---

181.   Luc de Fleurquin, 'Episcopal Collegiality in a Wider Europe' in Provost and Walf, *Collegiality put to the Test*, 122.

182.   See Henri de Lubac, *The Motherhood of the Church Followed by Particular Churches in the Universal Church* (San Francisco: Ignatius Press, 1982), 267–9.

183.   See Victorio Messori, *The Ratzinger Report: An Exclusive Interview on the State of the Church* (San Francisco: Ignatius Press, 1985), 61–2.

184.   See Alberigo and Komonchak, eds, *History of Vatican II: Mature Council*, 147–8.

185.   See Barbara Anne Cusack, 'The Diocesan Synod: A Teachable Moment in the Life of the Local Church', *The Jurist*, 63 (2003): 70–84.

186.   See Mariam Wijlens, 'Bishops and Their Relationship to a Local Church: A Canonical Perspective', *The Jurist*, 66 (2006): 211–41.

Diocesan synods in various guises have been a feature of church life for sixteen centuries. They are non-standing bodies comprising clerics and, since Vatican II, members of the laity. The bishop alone convokes (c. 462), suspends or dissolves them (c. 468). Their function is to assist the bishop for the good of the diocese, not to create a representative forum of the faithful. The Code commission saw the synod's main role as legislative at local level (in keeping with its history)[187] though confined to diocesan matters and obliged to remain consistent with church teaching. Canon 465 prescribes that there must be 'free discussion' of all matters raised but the votes of members are consultative only (c. 466). The Bishop is the Synod's sole legislator, so all synodal decrees and declarations require his express approval (c. 466). The Code commission 'indicated its presumption that legislative authority was a primary synod function,'[188] but according to a 1997 Curial Instruction on Diocesan Synods, the Synod is categorically '*not a college* with decisional capacity … votes are not intended as a binding majority decision'.[189]

Though not conciliar in origin the spirit of Vatican II is evid - ent in the extending of synod membership to the laity (cc. 460 and 463 §2) and of observer status to members of other denominations (c. 463 §3). Cusack describes it as a 'broad-based participatory structure'[190] but practice varies considerably throughout the church although such Synods are said to be regarded 'as important instruments in effecting conciliar renewal'.[191]

Compagnoni says that the 'monarchical episcopate' no longer fits the modern world and so,

> The synodal system, at both local and wider levels could take a substantial role in directing the life of the churches but in the sense that it would be a representative … organism of the

187. See *Communicationes*, 12 (1980), 315.
188. Cusack, 'The Diocesan Synod: A Teachable Moment in the Life of the Local Church', 71.
189. Congregation for Bishops and Congregation for the Evangelisation of Peoples, 'Instruction on Diocesan Synods' (1997), IV, 5.
190. Cusack, 'The Diocesan Synod: A Teachable Moment in the Life of the Local Church', 71.
191. See Congregation for Bishops and Congregation for the Evangelisation of Peoples, 'Instructions on Diocesan Synods' (1997), Prologue.

faithful. However its function is to guarantee the power of the bishops, to confirm their tenure ... and to sustain them in the exercise of their ministry.[192]

He also asserts that, 'Within the Catholic Church we observe sociologically if not dogmatically an even greater prominence of councils, pastoral, presbyteral and episcopal where the various components of the church are represented.'[193] It is true we see a greater prominence of canonical provision for participative fora but the fact that Ireland, a country with one of the largest Catholic majorities in the world, has not held a single diocesan Synod since Vatican II, may give some indication as to how little they contribute in reality.

Local participation in structured diocesan dialogue, where it has occurred at all, has not always been canonically intelligible, sometimes taking forms other than the synodal form provided for in *CIC*. Fearing that such assemblies were mistakenly perceived as *quasi* democratic structures representative of the People of God, the Congregation for Bishops, jointly with the Congregation for the Evangelisation of Peoples published, in 1997, an *Instruction on Diocesan Synods* designed to clarify the role of such Synods and to discourage informal diocesan assemblies from operating outside of the canonical norms for diocesan Synods.[194] The introduction to the *Instruction* specifically contextualises its discussion of diocesan synods within the Conciliar vision of the church summarised by Pope John Paul II in *SDL* as

> ... the doctrine whereby the church is presented as the People of God and its hierarchial authority as service; the further doctrine which portrays the church as a *communion* and then spells out the mutual relationships between the particular and the universal church, and between collegiality and primacy; and likewise, the doctrine by which all members of the People of God share, in a manner proper to each of them, in the threefold priestly, prophetic and kingly office of Christ (*Instruction*, Prologue).

---

192. Francesco Compagnoni, 'The Bishop and the Local Church', *The Jurist*, 66 (2006): 329.

193. Ibid.

194. See Congregation for Bishops and Congregation for Evangelisation of Peoples, 'Instruction on Diocesan Synods', Prologue.

In an 8,000 word document the word 'collegial' makes no further appearance. Instead a familiar line is drawn. Priests collaborate in Synods. Laity cooperate.[195] A Synod is not a diocesan parliament but,

> ... a priestly community, organically structured from its inception according to the will of its Founder, whose head, in every diocese, is the bishop, the visible source and foundation of unity and its sole representative. Thus any attempt to place the Synod in opposition to the bishop on the grounds of 'representation of the People of God' is contrary to the authentic order of ecclesial relations.[196]

The assumption that a forum which represented the People of God would necessarily be in opposition to the bishop would be worthy of serious analysis beyond the scope of this thesis. Some concession is made however to c. 212 for the *Instruction* specifically says that the faithful are to have the opportunity to express their opinions on what should be discussed at the Synod. Diocesan clergy likewise should be asked to make proposals in response to the 'pastoral challenges with which they are confronted' (Instruction I 2). It is however the bishop who decides the Synod agenda, bearing in mind the warning from the Instruction about the dangers of pressure groups and of creating false expectations (Instruction I 2). The dangers may have been internalised too deeply. Not a single diocesan Synod or official church body for that matter, managed to pre-empt civic society in alerting the church to the contemporary crises which have cost it so much financially and reputationally.

3.14 Conclusion

There is a wealth of information about collegial procedures in the General Norms of Book One of *CIC*. They are clear evidence that the church fully comprehends the nature of collegial procedures and the circumstances which call for such procedures. They emanate largely from pre-conciliar church practice as do the only two fully activated exemplars of effective episcopal Collegiality, the Ecumenical Council and the College of

---

195.   Ibid., I, 1.
196.   Ibid.

Cardinals. They favour juridic structures, encourage participative rather than solitary decision making where more serious decisions need to be made, generally favour majority voting as a means of eliciting the collegial will and show caution around the power and authority of a superior, consistently circumscribing it to ensure that his or her will is not imposed in place of the collegial will. Most of these canons owe little to the principle of conciliar collegiality though they are indebted to the general need to modernise CIC/17 where most had rough equivalents. Their logic is not followed through when it comes to the provisions made in CIC for conciliar collegiality. Instead that logic is routinely avoided, circumvented or ignored while the word collegiality is liberally used to describe ecclesial structures which would not pass the test of collegiality set down by the General Norms. Conciliar collegiality is ironically therefore a pale imitation of pre-conciliar collegiality, a glossy façade behind which lies something of an anti-climax.

CIC's provisions for new forms of effective juridic conciliar collegiality are not only modest but make no practical change to the pre-Vatican II situation beyond relabelling the convoked College of Bishops to make it coterminous with Ecumenical Councils. Conciliar and canonical provision for more extensive use of the College of Bishops' power of universal church governance is made in principle only and has never been activated. The episcopacy has made no request for change in the *status quo* through any of the bodies which give it vertical access to the Pope.

Affective episcopal collegiality has been developed with the help of CIC into a jumble of juridically chaotic entities, in particular the Synod of Bishops and Episcopal Conferences, which have no deliberative powers in regard to the universal church and no clear legal relationship with the College of Bishops. They do however have the capacity to emasculate both Ecumenical and particular Councils (both of which have deliberative powers) and to contribute to greater rather than lesser centralised primatial control, since their juridic status is weak. Given that the Curia is a tool of primatial authority, attempts to characterise it as a vehicle of episcopal collegiality lack juridic credibility and leave it as constitutionally problematic in CIC as it was in

CIC/17. It remains a hybrid institution, functioning in a juridic limbo as both an executive and legislature aligned juridically to the papacy but not to the College of Bishops except in the technical sense that the Pope is Head of the College.

Collegiality at sub-episcopal level involves the slack use of the word to describe structures and fora, practices and procedures which have moved towards greater participation and inclusivity by the faithful. They are most evolved within religious institutes where they are unequivocally designed to promote greater representation and democracy among the members. Insofar as participative structures involve the laity at any level of the church, they are of modest even minimal proportions and what is more they are explicitly not designed to promote representative participation or democratic structures but rather to promote ecclesial communion through assisting the pastors and bishops who alone canonically have the right to teach and govern. That they are quite timid affairs is evident from their proven inability to be conduits for dealing with serious local problems e.g. clerical abuse, which instead were left to fester until they combusted spectacularly in the secular sphere bringing in their wake an avalanche of problems that many dioceses and episcopal conferences are still coming awkwardly to terms with.

Beal has claimed that the church is now dangerously close to 'a perfect storm' caused, but only in part by the 'howling gale' of protest at the revelations of abuse and the concomitant systemic institutional failures to deal appropriately with abusers and victims. The other contributors to this converging storm are in his view, 'the long-standing resentment by the lay faithful (but also and more quietly the lower clergy) at the lack of accountability, transparency and opportunities for participation in church governance' and the 'turbulent current whose leading edge has only recently appeared on our ecclesial radar … the historic resentment of the lower clergy and to a lesser extent their lay supporters at allegedly arbitrary and capricious treatment of them by diocesan bishops'.[197] Whether this spells a yearning still for the

---

197. See John Beal, 'Weathering the Perfect Storm' in Stephen J. Pope, ed., *Common Calling: The Laity and the Governance of the Catholic Church* (Washington DC: Georgetown University Press, 2004), 166–`7.

Council's *novus habitus mentis* or spells the end of it is too early to say but with the passage of fifty eventful years since Vatican II and over twenty-five since *CIC*, one is entitled to wonder whither collegiality?

CHAPTER FOUR

Quo Vadis? Whither Collegiality?

Pre-conciliar collegiality is clear. There wasn't much of it, except at Ecumenical Councils and when the College of Cardinals acted in an interregnum but what there was had clearly delineated laws, juridically straight lines of authority and powers capable of plain description. By comparison post-conciliar collegiality is chaotic, with little evident direction in its development or jurido/constitutional rigour in its structure. The part of *CIC* which owes most to pre-conciliar law knows exactly what collegiality implies. The part which owes most to Vatican II is unable to come to terms with what collegiality implies.

Today the best experts of the church cannot coherently explain the church's governance structures or their juridic infrastructure. This is largely thanks to Vatican II, which failed to articulate clear guidelines for the future development of conciliar collegiality or church governance at any level. No post-conciliar body was charged with resolving the conciliar ambiguities, consequently the 1983 Code of Canon Law was forced to enact basic constitutional structures of governance that were inherently unstable and inchoate. Left to their own devices they could never be anything else. *CIC* ends up with a bi-furcated, even bi-polar collegiality, one sourced from *CIC/17* that is straightforward and the other from Vatican II that is anything but. Whether this situation is Örsy's 'slow burn' leading to a rich harvest or a directionless meandering leading in circles, is hard to tell. Örsy says, 'As the council fathers struggled with the process of conversion, the church at large is doing the same today.'[1]

Green remarks that Conciliar insights will '... positively influence the church's life and mission only if they are incarnated in institutional structures ... Canonical structures assist a

---

1. Ladislas Örsy, 'Law for Life', *The Jurist*, 67 (2007): 37.

community in implementing its theological vision'.[2] He believes conciliar collegiality needs those structures 'to assist the
community in making this multifaceted doctrine a lived reality
... if we are seriously to "receive" Vatican II, theologians and
canonists must continually collaborate in assessing whether our
structures need to be so adapted that they may assist the community more effectively in achieving the unity of the church of
Christ'.[3]

These ambiguities might have been unproblematic in a
church characterised by an uneducated, obedient and deferen-
tial laity. They are no longer unproblematic for this is a singularly
bad moment historically to be shrouded in such juridic vagueness. The church, and in particular authority in the church, is
under probative, forensic, widespread scrutiny as never before,
not to mention ground-breaking civil investigations in several
jurisdictions. Indeed a new generation has grown up against a
relentless backdrop of well-grounded scholarly criticism of the
church based on thorough-going investigations particularly in
relation to clerical child abuse. Somewhat late in the day church
protocols on that subject have improved considerably in some
jurisdictions and the Pope has insisted that all dioceses throughout the church make child protection provision a priority. The
ground-breaking Conference on Child Protection hosted by the
Gregorian University in Rome in February 2012 has helped to
draw attention to the problem throughout the universal church
and to promote a universal best practice response. However
these developments have only served to underline that despite
many claims about modernising conciliar outcomes the structures of church governance were not in fact markedly updated
in the twentieth century, leaving the church one among very
few global institutions not to have been updated from within
or without. The hopes that Vatican II would create a pathway to
reform of governance have not yet been realised and the road
map it left is barely intelligible.

The coming years will reveal the extent to which Conciliar
and post-Conciliar failures may have already hollowed out

---

2.   See Thomas J. Green, 'Collegiality in the Church: Theology and Canon
      Law: Editor's Introduction', *The Jurist*, 64 (2004): 1.
3.   Ibid., 2–3.

communion along with trust. Marco Politi, Vatican correspondent of *La Repubblica* has argued that recent vocal episcopal dissent from the Pope's proposed readmission of Lefebvrists and the appointment of the Bishop of Linz, amount to evidence of a 'new age of dissent' and 'an underlying tension that could easily ignite ... beneath the surface of Roman power – as under a volcano – one can hear ominous rumblings.' The 'heart of the crisis' is in his view 'the failure to implement collegiality'.[4]

It is not for this study to prescribe how greater juridic coherence might be achieved or conciliar collegiality brought to more practical fruition than hitherto, though I hope it provokes discussion on possibilities. There are many varieties of organisational models throughout the world, few of which nowadays match the solitariness of the church's primatial rule. There is a wealth of suggestions from canonists, theologians and others about possible models or the more advanced development of existing models. There is a growing body of criticism of the *status quo* but equally it has many staunch defenders. There is no forum in the church for determining the views of the People of God on the subject of governance and collegiality or virtually anything else for that matter, despite the clear provisions of c. 212 §3. They have never been asked their views and there is an abhorrence at the centre of the dangers of being governed by opinion polls. Ironically the absence of formal collegial structures and the strength of public civic discourse have left the church very exposed to and regularly engaged in fire-fighting just such publicly expressed angst. Often the reaction from the centre has been one of surprise on hearing the views from the circumference. In a collegial church where information was free-flowing horizontally and vertically, there should be no such surprises.

I have tried to show the strengths, weaknesses and contradictions of the very different models of collegiality provided for in *CIC*. I have concluded that they demonstrate that currently the church lacks an obvious idea of where it is going in terms of collegial governance. The dynamic at the centre, where all juridic initiative is located, is still strongly pro-primatial and

---

4.   Marco Politi, 'The Church's New Age of Dissent', *The Tablet*, 21 March (2009): 5.

hostile to broadening the kind of collegiality already exercised in the pre-conciliar church.

Peters says 'codified ecclesiastical law is still in its infancy; less than five per cent of church history has been spent under an integrated code'.[5] But the Code itself is not the primary problem, though it is the conduit for the problem. The church is in effect, arguably, constitutionally incoherent. It has a governing Head, the nature of whose authority, though divinely instituted, is opaque; that authority is linked to the College of the Apostles and to Peter, but precisely how is not clear. The College of Bishops has full and supreme power over the universal church but how that power relates to papal power remains undifferentiated and untested except in conciliar format. The college has not met or actively expressed its collegial will since 1965. The Pope, the Synod of Bishops and the College of Cardinals are all said to 'represent' the College of Bishops but in fact only the Pope does so canonically. No-one knows for sure when he acts in the name of the college and when he acts personally. The Curia, which looks like a Civil Service, acts like a government but on what authority? It has no juridic relationship whatsoever to the College of Bishops, yet as an executive branch of government it might be legitimately expected to have a clear line of reporting accountability to a body charged by Christ with the full and supreme governance of the church. It reports and accounts exclusively to the Pope.

Discussion within the church at every level is generally heavily circumscribed and controlled to avoid dissent. Rightly or wrongly it looks as if the centre does not want to hear bad news or to face challenges from the circumference. It looks as if *communio* is believed to thrive through passive obedience and silence on any subject of controversy. Yet many commentators think the opposite, that the church is being weakened by the absence of healthy flows upwards and downwards of information and opinion.

In the early part of the twentieth century less than ten per cent of the nations of the world were democracies. Today that figure is closer to sixty-five per cent. The pace of change has

---

5.   Peters, ed., *CIC/17*. xxx.

been as relentless as it has been incredible with much of it impossible to predict. The church has been challenged by both the
changes and the speed at which life is being transformed. Those
who live in the world's growing number of democracies have
considerable freedom of expression in the civil sphere but highly-
restricted freedom of expression in the religious sphere.
Reconciling both spheres can be difficult; the same discussion
may be perceived in one sphere as acceptable freedom of expression and unacceptable disrespect for the teaching magisterium in the other. Church teaching on clerical celibacy, ordination
of women, gay marriage, admission of divorced and remarried
Catholics to the sacraments, is not necessarily an expression of
the views of Catholics generally as opinion polls in Ireland have
shown.[6] Church teaching on birth control is so widely ignored
that some canonical commentators question whether it can be
said to have been 'received' and therefore validated by the faithful. The heterocentricity of Catholic teaching (and indeed other
faiths) is now being looked at critically in the light of the deadly
consequences of homophobic bullying, with research, mainly in
the United States, showing a tragic link between male youth suicide and homosexuality.[7] The future impact on Catholic schools
is a question already being pondered. Could church teaching on
homosexuality be the new psychological child abuse issue of the
coming decade?

Human beings have never been strangers to change but in
the developed world there have been advances on an unimagin-
able scale in many fields of endeavour especially in the post-
conciliar latter part of the twentieth century. The church which
is still in the process of adapting to the Council after fifty years,
exists in a world which has shown an amazing capacity to adapt
much more rapidly to things infinitely more complex than
collegiality. Much of Vatican II's discussion of governance, collegiality and the People of God occurred as the world was merely
on the cusp of these changes. The educated laity was then an

---

6.   Amarach Consulting, *Report conducted for the Association of Catholic
      Priests* (2012), available from www.associationofcatholicpriests.ie. [Accessed
      12.4.2012.]

7.   Report of the Secretary's Task Force on Youth Suicide, vol. 3: Prevention
      and Intervention in Youth Suicide.

elite, not the mass phenomenon it is today. Communications media and technologies lacked the immediacy and massive global reach they currently have. The role of women in society was considerably more circumscribed than it is now. And there are many more examples. Just as the tide of secular empires ebbed, leaving the church and its then Code of Canon Law in need of the modernisation begun at Vatican II, so today's world of increasingly democratic and inclusive secular structures makes solitary centralised authorities look like an ebb tide. Those who argue that centralised primatialism avoids the disunity and conflict of more collegial denominations and protects *communio* would do well to examine closely the mote of emptying pews and bewildered faithful in their own eye.

The word 'collegiality' captured something of an incipient impulse towards greater inclusivity and respect for the voice and views of the individual. It came to be associated with the *novus habitus mentis* within the church which would parallel, though in different ways, the new world that was emerging. Through over-usage, abuse, general carelessness and failure to bring the concept fully home, it has become a word of debased coinage in ecclesial terms. As a prime conciliar concept in which it was hoped could be found the live seed of the *novus habitus mentis* it has delivered, in practical terms, almost exactly nothing other than unrealised possibilities. For those who hoped for greater co-governance of the universal church between the Pope and the College of Bishops, it has been a journey of disappointment since the Council. On the other side of the equation the Council fathers who worried that 'collegiality' would be a runaway horse that would do untold damage to the primacy of the Pope and the unity of the church need not have worried. Other things not thought of at the Council, all of them internal, have inflicted appalling unforeseen, though avoidable damage but collegiality is not among them. Secrecy and solitary rule have inflicted the worst of it, the very things collegiality could have been and still could be a bulwark against.

The ambiguity of the Council in relation to widening effective episcopal collegiality translated into inertia in *CIC*. The Code commission and *CIC* took endless pains to ensure that outside of the Pope himself no clear mechanism would exist to fan Örsy's slow burn to a flame. A quiescent episcopacy failed to carry forward the conciliar agenda on episcopal collegiality with any enthusiasm. As the bishops dispersed throughout the world after the Council, the conciliar momentum behind episcopal collegiality dispersed too never to be regained. By default an excluded and largely trained-to-be and expected-to-be passive laity also contributed little. Having no forum through which to speak on such matters their views went unheard. Yet the conciliar call to greater lay involvement in the church superficially looks to have fared better than episcopal collegiality. It is hard to say whether the minor changes that have drawn a few more members of the faithful into a deeper and wider sharing of the three *munera* can be ascribed to the Council or to other ambient secular and ecclesial forces which have been at play over the last fifty years and which have reduced clerical manpower in many developed countries. Certainly the spirit of the Council and the letter of *CIC* helped facilitate greater inclusivity but within well demarcated limits which, along with weak juridical status, ensured there could never be any meaningful debate on doctrine or policy. Those who hoped for a more open engagement and who now see the local and universal church as more dithering than decisive in the face of very public problems, are faced with a logjam which constitutionally only the Pope can release.

However does any of this matter? The enduring nature of the church, its service over two millennia, its formidable and unequalled contribution at local and international level, might well, in some quarters, justify maintaining the *status quo*. Yet the questions would still be posed whether this is the model of governance that either Christ or the Council intended and whether it can realistically enhance and maintain the communion of the People of God into the future? These questions at the heart of the hottest dispute at the Council have become the arena of least development. After two millennia of Revelation, extensive discussions by the most distinguished theological scholars, the entire episcopacy, two Popes at the Second Vatican Council and three Popes since, not to mention the discussions at the first Vatican Council, the best that can be said about our understanding of the juridical nature of the College of Bishops, its relationship with papal authority, the basic governance structure of the church and the role of collegiality at episcopal and other church levels, is that, the Holy Spirit notwithstanding, we await further and fuller clarification. No body at official level within the church is currently working towards that clarification but the forces of ecumenical dialogue, of crisis management, of sustained and often strident debate in the civic, canonical and theological spheres have a momentum which is impinging asymmetrically on both the centre and the circumference of the church from outside and inside.

We have seen it argued that conciliar collegiality may benefit in the long run from a definitional nebulousness so that it can grow, and develop over time. Equally we have heard the opposite, that the conciliar inability to give form and structure then or since has been fatal to conciliar collegiality. So are we in a process of ongoing conversion or irreconcilable division, a journey towards greater collegiality or enduring primatialism in an increasingly fragmented church? Some might argue, whither collegiality, whither the church. With the golden anniversary of the Council upon us, Mickens, in contemplating whether the new wine of the Second Vatican Council was put into old wineskins, asks if the anniversary could be 'rather than a celebration of *aggiornamento*, or updating, a time of mourning for lost opportunity?'[8]

Perhaps what is needed to oxygenate the 'slow burn' so that the church can be truly a light to the world is the fuel, commanded by Christ himself in the greatest commandment of all, to love one another. It was Pope John Paul II who stated in the introduction to the 1983 Code of Canon Law that the Code is a complement to the teaching of the Second Vatican Council and must transpose the image of the church described by conciliar doctrine while attributing always primacy to love, grace and the charisms.

De Chardin says it elegantly: 'Some day after mastering the winds, the waves, the tides and gravity [we] shall harness ... the energies of love. And then for the second time in the history of the world we shall have discovered fire.'[9]

---

8.   Robert Mickens, 'The Church in Disarray', *The Tablet*, 25 February 2012.
9.   Teilhard de Chardin, *Toward the Future* (London: Collins, 1975), 86–7.

Wind and waves are pounding us. Tides are swollen and angry. Once a long time ago a God-man invited us to push out into the deep, where there are no safe bunkers just the adventure of seeing what faith in God and love can accomplish in a world that needs healing from all the hurts that life, nature and human beings inflict, from the enigma of life and the enigma of death. He placed his trust in frail humanity, in Peter, a far from outstanding man who eventually found his strength in facing his many weaknesses, not on his own but with Christ's help. In this moment those who ardently desire a truly collegial church have no option but to look to Peter's successor to push out into the deep, to open the closed doors and let the future in. 'Quo vadis?' Christ is said to have once asked Peter. The answer changed the course of history. The same question is being asked again.

162

Sources

Anglo–Roman Catholic International Commission, 'The Gift of Authority' (1998).

Benedict XV. Apostolic Constitution *Providentissima Mater Ecclesia*. 27 May 1917, *AAS* 9/2, 1917, 11–521. English translation in E. N. Peters (ed.), *The 1917 Pio-Benedictine Code of Canon Law*, San Francisco, Ignatius Press, 2001, 21–24.

Benedict XVI, 'Letter of His Holiness Pope Benedict XVI to the Bishops of the Catholic Church Concerning the Remission of the Excommunication of the Four Bishops Consecrated by Archbishop Lefebvre' (10 March 2009), www.vatican.va/holy_father/benedict_xvi/letters/2009/documents/hf_b en-xvi_let_20090310_remissione-scomunica_en.html. [Accessed 01.4.2009.]

Berger, Adolf, *Encyclopaedic Dictionary of Roman Law*, Philadelphia: The American Philosophical Society, 1953.

Brown, Lesley, ed., *New Shorter Oxford English Dictionary*, Oxford: Clarendon Press, 1993.

Burke, John, *A Dictionary of Canon Law*, Akure, Nigeria: Don Bosco Publications, 2004.

Catechism of the Catholic Church, 2nd Edition, United States Conference of Catholic Bishops, 1997.

Codex Iuris canonici auctoritate Ioannis Pauli PP. II promulgatus fontium annotatione et indice analytico-alphabetico auctus. English translation from Libreria Editrice Vaticana, www.vatican.va/archive/eng1104/_index.html. [Accessed 01.7.2008.]

Code of Canon Law: Latin–English Edition, New English translation, prepared under the auspices of the Canon Law society of America, Washington, Canon Law Society of America, 1999.

Code of Canon Law, new rev. English translation prepared by the Canon Law Society of Great Britain and Ireland, in association with the Canon Law Society of Australia and New Zealand and the Canadian Canon Law Society, London, HarperCollins, 1997.

Codex Iuris Canonici Pii X Pontificis maximi iussu digestus Benedicti Papae XV auctoritate promulgatus, Typis Polyglottis Vaticanis, 1917, English translation E. N. Peters (ed.), *The 1917 Pio Benedictine Code of Canon Law*, San Francisco, Ignatius press, 2001.

Commission of Investigation, 'Report into the Catholic Archdiocese of Dublin', Dublin: Department of Equality, Justice and Law Reform, July 2009, www.justice.ie/en/JELR/Pages/PB09000504. [Accessed 14.04.2010.]

Congregation for Bishops and Congregation for the Evangelisation of Peoples. 'Instructions on Diocesan Synods', 8 July 1997 in *AAS*, 89 (1997), 706–21. English translation from Libreria Editrice Vaticana, www.vatican.va/roman _curia/congregations/cbishops/documents/rc_con_cbishops_doc_200411 18_diocesan-synods-1997_en.html. [Accessed 05.4.2009.]

Congregation for the Clergy, *Instruction on Certain Questions Regarding the Collaboration of the Non-Ordained Faithful in the Ministry of Priests Ecclesiae de Mysterio* (15 August 1997), *AAS*, 89 (1997), 852–77. English translation from Libreria Editrice Vaticana, www.vatican.va/roman_ curia/pontifical_councils/laity/documents/rc_con_interdic_doc_15081997_en.html. [Accessed 01.9.2008.]

Congregation for Doctrine and Faith, *Il Primato del Successore di Pietro*, Atti del
    Simposio teologico, Rome, 2–4 December 1996, Libreria Editrice Vaticana,
    Vatican City, 1998, English translation in *Origins*, 28, 1998–9, 207–16.
Ecumenical Patriarch Bartholomew I, Speech to the XII Ordinary General
    Assembly of the Synod of Bishops, 26 October 2008, *Synodus Episcoporum
    Bulletin*, Holy See Press Office, English edition, www.vatican.va/news_ser-
    vices/press/sinodo/documents/bollettino_22_xii-ordinaria-2008/02_in-
    glese/b30_02.html. [Accessed 05.4.2009.]
Faith and Order Commission of the World Council of Churches, 'Paper No. 198.
    *The Nature and Mission of the Church: A Stage on the Way to a Common
    Statement*, December 2005.
John Paul II, apostolic constitution *Sacrae Disciplinae Leges*, 25 January 1983 in
    AAS, 75/II (1983), VII–XIV, English translation in *The Code of Canon Law, pre-
    pared by The Canon Law Society of Great Britain & Ireland in association with The
    Canon Law Society of Australia & New Zealand and The Canadian Canon Law
    Society*, London: HarperCollins, 1997, xi–xvi.
    — apostolic constitution *Pastor Bonus* 28 June 1988 in *AAS*, 80 (1988),
      841–912. English translation from Libreria Editrice Vaticana, www.vati-
      can.va/holy_father/john_paul_ii/apost_constitutions/documents/hf_
      jp-ii_apc_19880628_pastor-bonus-index_en.html.
    — post Synodal apostolic exhortation on the mission and vocation of the lay
      faithful *Christifideles Laici*, 30 December 1988 in *AAS*, 81 (1989), 393–521.
      English translation from Libreria Editrice Vaticana, www.vatican.va/
      holy_father/john_paul_ii/apost_exhortations/documents/hf_jp-
      ii_exh_30121988_christifideles-laici_en.html. [Accessed 05.4.2009.]
    — discourse of His Holiness John Paul II to the Council of the General
      Secretariat of the Synod of Bishops, 30 April 1983 in *L'Osservatore
      Romano: Weekly Edition in English*, 23 May 1983, 5.
    — Encyclical *Ut Unum Sint*, 25 May 1995 in *AAS*, 87 (1995), 921–82. English
      translation from Libreria Editrice Vaticana, www.vatican.va/edocs/
      eng0221/_index.html. [Accessed 01.9.2009.]
    — apostolic letter issued *motu proprio, Apostolos Suos*, 21 May 1998. English
      translation from Libreria Editrice Vaticana, www.vatican.va/holy_fa-
      ther/john_paul_ii/motu_proprio/documents/hf_jp-ii_motu-pro-
      prio_22071998_apostolos-suos_en.html.
    — Homily at the Conclusion of the Synod Of Bishops, 27 October 2001
      www.vatican.va/holy_father/john_paul_ii/homilies/2001/documents/h
      f_jpii_hom_20011027_closing-synod_en.html. [Accessed 01.10.2008.]
    — apostolic exhortation *Pastores Gregis*, 16 October 2003 in *AAS*, 96 (2004),
      825–924, English translation from Libreria Editrice Vaticana, www.vati-
      can.va/holy_father/john_paul_ii/apost_exhortations/documents/hf_j
      p-ii_exh_20031016_pastores-gregis_en.html.
Paul VI, *'Discorso Ai Partecipanti', Persona e Ordinamento nella Chiesa*, Atti del II
    Congreso Internaziolale di Diritto Canonico. Milano 10–16 Settembre 1973
    in *L'Osservatore Romano*, September 17–18, 1973.
    — See Paul VI, Apostolic Letter written *motu proprio, Ecclesiae Sanctae*, 6
      August 1966 in *AAS* 58 (1966), 757–87. English translation from Libreria
      Editrice Vaticana, www.vatican.va/holy_father/paul_vi/motu_proprio/
      documents/hf_p-vi_motu-proprio_19660806_ecclesiae-sanctae
      _en.html. [Accessed 01.3.2009.]
    — *motu proprio, Apostolica Sollicitudo*, 15 September 1965 in *AAS*, 57
      (1965), 775–780. English translation from Libreria Editrice Vaticana,

www.vatican.va/holy_father/paul_vi/motu_proprio/documents/hf_
p-vi_motu-proprio_19690624_sollicitudo-omnium-ecclesiarum_lt.html.
[Accessed 05.4.2009.]

— Sunday Angelus, 22 September 1974, Synod of Bishops, Holy See Press
Office available, www.vatican.va/news_services/press/documentazione
/documents/sinodo_indice_en.ht. [Accessed 05.4.2009.]

Pius XII, encyclical *Fidei Donum*, 21 April 1957 in *AAS* XLIX (1957), 225–48.
English translation from Libreria Editrice Vaticana, www.papalencycli-
cals.net/Pius12/P12fidei.html. [Accessed 05.4.2009.]

Pontificia Commission Codicis Iuris Canonici Recognocendo, Pontifical
Commission for the Revision of the Code of Canon Law, Plenary Session,
20–9 October 1981.

Stelten, Leo F., *Dictionary of Ecclesiastical Latin: With an Appendix of Latin
Expressions Defined and Clarified,* Peabody, Mass.: Hendrickson, 1995.

United Nations General Assembly, 'Universal Declaration of Human Rights', 1948.

Vatican II, 'Constitution on the Sacred Liturgy *Sacrosanctum Concilium*', 4
December 1963 in *AAS*, 56 (1964), 97–134, English translation in Flannery,
*Vatican Council II: The Basic Sixteen Documents: Constitutions, Decrees,
Declaration* (Dublin, Ireland: Dominican Publications, 1996), 117–161.

— Declaration on Religious Liberty *Dignitatis Humanae*, 7 December 1963
in *AAS*, 58 (1966), 929–41. English translation in Flannery, 551–68.

— Decree on Ecumenism *Unitatis Redintegratio*, 21 November 1964 in *AAS*,
58 (1966), 929–41. English translation in Flannery, 499–523.

— Dogmatic Constitution on the Church *Lumen gentium*, 22 November
1964 in *AAS*, 57 (1964), 5–75. English translation in Flannery, 1–95.

— Declaration on Christian Education *Gravissimum Educationis*, 28 October
1965 in *AAS*, 58 (1965), 728–39. English translation in Flannery, 575–91.

— Declaration on the Relation of the Church to Non-Christian Religions
Nostra Aetate, 28 October 1965 in *AAS*, 58 (1966), 740–5. English translation in Flannery, 569–74.

— Decree Concerning the Pastoral Office of Bishops in the Church; *Christus
Dominus*, 28 October 1965 in *AAS*, 58 (1966), 673–96. English translation
in Flannery, 283–315.

— Decree on the up-to-date Renewal of Religious Life *Perfectae Caritas* (28
October 1965) in *AAS*, 57 (1964), 5–75. English translation in Flannery,
385–401.

— Decree on the Apostolate of Lay People *Apostolicam Actuositatem*, 18
November 1965 in *AAS*, 58 (1966), 837–64. English translation in
Flannery, 403–42.

— Decree on the Catholic Eastern Churches *Orientalium Ecclesiarum*, 21
November 1965 in *AAS*, 57 (1965), 76–9. English translation in Flannery,
525–38.

— Decree on the Mass Media *Inter Mirifica*, 4 December 1963 in *AAS*, 56
(1964), 145–57. English translation in Flannery, 539–550.

— Decree on the Church's Missionary Activity *Ad Gentes Divinitus*, 7
December 1965 in *AAS*, 58 (1966), 947–90, English Translation in
Flannery, 443–97.

— Pastoral Constitution on the Church in the Modern World *Gaudium
et Spes*, 7 December 1965 in *AAS*, 58 (1966) 713. English translation in
Flannery, 163–282.

— Decree on the Ministry and Life of Priests *Presbyterorum Ordinis*, 7
December 1965 in *AAS*, 58 (1966), 991–1024. English translation in
Flannery, 317–64.

SOURCES   165

— Decree on the Training of Priests *Optatam Totius*, 28 October 1966 in
    AAS, 58 (1966), 713–17. English translation in Flannery, 365–84.

BOOKS

Alberigo, Guissepe, and Joseph A. Komonchak, eds, *History of Vatican II: The
    Formation of the Council's Identity: First Period and Intersession October
    1962–September 1963*, vol. II, New York: Leuven: Orbis/Peeters, 1997.
—   eds, *History of Vatican II: The Mature Council; Second Period and
    Intersession: September 1963–September 1964*, vol. III, New York: Leuven:
    Orbis/Peeters, 2006.
—   eds, *History of Vatican II*, vol. IV: New York: Leuven: Orbis/Peeters, 2004.
Allen Jr, John L., *Cardinal Ratzinger: The Vatican's Enforcer of the Faith*, New York:
    Continuum, 2000.
Arrieta, Juan Ignacio, *Governance Structures within the Catholic Church*, Gratianus
    Series. Montreal: Wilson and Lafleur, 2000.
Beal, John P., James A. Coriden, and Thomas J. Green, eds, *New Commentary on
    the Code of Canon Law*, New York, NY/Mahwah, NJ: Paulist Press, 2000.
—   eds, *New Commentary on the Code of Canon Law*, New York, NY/ Mahwah,
    NJ: Paulist Press, 2000.
Caparros, Ernest, Michel Thiériault, and John Thorn, eds, *Code of Canon Law
    Annotated*, Montreal: Wilson & Lafleur Limitée, 2004.
Coriden, James A., *An Introduction to Canon Law: Revised*, Mahwah, NJ: Paulist
    Press, 2004.
Cotter, Elizabeth M., *The General Chapter in a Religious Institute: With Particular
    Reference to IBVM Loreto Branch*, Bern: Peter Lang, 2008.
De Broucker, José, *The Suenens Dossier: The Case for Collegiality*, Notre Dame,
    Indiana: Fides, 1970.
De Chardin, Teilhard, *Toward the Future*, London: Collins, 1975.
Dulles, Avery Robert, *The Catholicity of the Church*, Oxford: Clarendon Press, 1987.
Eschenberg, T., *Über autorität*, Frankfurt, Suhrkamp, 1976.
Flannery, Austin, *Vatican Council II: The Basic Sixteen Documents: Constitutions,
    Decrees, Declaration* (Northport NY, Dublin: Costello; Dominican Publications,
    1996).
Fransen, Piet F., ed., *Authority in the Church*, Leuven: Leuven University Press, 1983.
Ghirlanda, Gianfranco, *Il Diritto Nella Chiesa, Mistero Di Comunione: Compendio
    Di Diritto Ecclesiale*, Cinisello Balsamo, Milano. Roma: Edizioni Paoline,
    Editrice Pontificia Università Gregoriana, 1990.
Granfield, Patrick, and Peter C. Phan, *The Gift of the Church: A Textbook
    Ecclesiology in Honor of Patrick Granfield OSB*, Collegeville, Minn.: Liturgical
    Press, 2000.
Grootaers, Jan, 'Une restauration de la theologie de l'episcopat', Contribution du
    Cardinal Alfrink a la preparation de Vatican II, *'Glaube im process. Christsein
    nach dem II Vatikanum.'* Fur Karl Rahner, ed. Elmar Klinger, Klaus Wittstadt
    (Freiburg-Basel-Vienna 1984).
Heaney, Seamus, *New Selected Poems 1966–1987*, London: Faber and Faber, 1990.
Kearney, Fiona, ed., *Modern American Paintings from the NYU Art Collection*
    (Cork: Glucksman, 2004), 95.
Komonchak, Joseph A., 'Introduction' in *The Motherhood of the Church*, edited by
    Henri de Lubac: Ignatius Press, 1982.
Komonchak, Joseph A., Mary Collins, and Dermot A. Lane, *The New Dictionary of
    Theology*, Collegeville, Minn.: Liturgical Press, 1990.

Küng, Hans, *Reforming the Church Today: Keeping Hope Alive*, trs P. Heinegg with F. McDonagh et al., New York: The Crossroad Publishing Company, 1990.

Lakeland, Paul, *The Liberation of the Laity: In Search of an Accountable Church*, New York: Continuum, 2003.

Lombardia Diaz, Pedro, *Lecciones De Derecho Canonico: Introduccion Derecho Constitucional. Parte General* (Spanish Edition). Madrid: Grupo Anaya Comercial, 1984.

Lubac, Henri de, *The Motherhood of the Church Followed by Particular Churches in the Universal Church*, San Francisco: Ignatius Press, 1982.

Mannion, Gerard, *The Vision of John Paul II: Assessing His Thought and Influence*, Collegeville, Minn.: Liturgical Press, 2008.

Marzoa, Angel, Jorge Miras, and Rafael Rodriguez-Ocana, eds, *Exegetical Commentary on the Code of Canon Law*, edited by Faculty of Canon Law University of Navarre, 5 vols, Gratianus, Montreal; Chicago: Wilson & Lafleur; MidWest Theological Union, 2004.

Messori, Victorio, *The Ratzinger Report: An Exclusive Interview on the State of the Church*, San Francisco: Ignatius Press, 1985.

Oakley, Francis, *The Conciliarist Tradition: Constitutionalism in the Catholic Church, 1300-1870*, Oxford; New York: Oxford University Press, 2003.

Oakley, Francis and Bruce Russett, *Governance, Accountability and the Future of the Catholic Church*, New York: Continuum, 2004.

Peters, Edward N., *Incrementa in Progressu 1983 Codicis Iuris Canonici: With a Multilingual Introduction (English, Francais, Italiano, Espanol, Deutsch, Polski)*, Collection Gratianus, Montreal, Quebec: Wilson & Lafleur, 2005.

— *The 1917 Pio-Benedictine Code of Canon Law*, ed., San Francisco, Ignatius Press, 2001.

Pope, Stephen J., ed., *Common Calling: The Laity and the Governance of the Catholic Church*, Washington DC: Georgetown University Press, 2004.

Provost, James H., and Knut Walf, eds, 'Collegiality put to the Test', *Concilium*, London, Philadelphia: SCM Press; Trinity Press International, 1990.

Quinn, John R., *The Reform of the Papacy: The Costly Call to Christian Unity. Ut Unum Sint: Studies on Papal Primacy*, New York: The Crossroad Publishing Company, 1999.

Ratzinger, Joseph Cardinal, *Called to Communion: Understanding the Church Today*, trs Adrian Walker. San Francisco: Ignatius Press, 1991.

— *Church, Ecumenism and Politics: New Endeavours in Ecclesiology*, San Francisco: Ignatius Press, 2008.

— *Das Neue Volk Gottes. Entwürfe Zur Ekklesiologie.* Dusseldorf: Patmos, 1969.

Reese, Thomas J., ed., *Episcopal Conferences: Historical, Canonical and Theological Studies*, Washington DC: Georgetown University Press, 1989.

Schatz, Klaus, *Papal primacy: from its origins to the present*, trs John A. Otto and Linda M. Moloney, Collegeville, Minn.: Liturgical Press, 1996.

Schreer, Werner and Georg Steins eds, *Auf neue Art Kirche Sein: Wirklichkeiten-Herausfoderungen-Wandlungen*, Munich: Bernward bei Don Bosco, 1999.

Sharkey, Michael ed., *International Theological Commission: Texts and Document* (San Francisco: Ignatius Press, 1987), 32–5.

Sullivan SJ, Francis J., *Magisterium. Teaching Authority in the Catholic Church*, Dublin: Gill and Macmillan, 1983.

Tagle, Luis Antonio G., *Episcopal Collegiality and Vatican II: The Influence of Paul VI*, Landas Monographs. Manila, Philippines: Loyola School of Theology, 2004.

Tanner, Norman, *Was the Church Too Democratic? Councils, Collegiality and the Church's Future*, Bangalore: Dharmaram Publications, 2003.

Weber, Max, *Economy and Society: An Outline of Interpretive Sociology*, ed., Claus Wittich and Ephraim Fischoff Guenther Roth, Berkeley: University of California Press, 1978.

Wilde, Melissa J., *Vatican II: A Sociological Analysis of Religious Change*, Princeton: Princeton University Press, 2007.

ARTICLES

Allen Jr., John L., 'Collegiality vs. Centralization Dominates Synod, *National Catholic Reporter*, 12 October 2001 www.natcath.org/NCR_Online/archives2/2001d/101201/101201f.html. [Accessed 06.5.2009.]

Clifford, Catherine, 'Emerging Consensus on Collegiality and Catholic Ecumenical Responsibility', *The Jurist*, 64 (2004): 332–60.

Coccopalmerio, Francesco, 'The Role of the Legislator in the Church' in *Annual Conference of the Canon law Society of Great Britain and Ireland May 5–9*, Rome, 2008.

Compagnoni, Francesco, 'The Bishop and the Local Church', *The Jurist*, 66 (2006): 329–31.

Coriden, James A., 'The Synod of Bishops: Episcopal Collegiality Still Seeks Adequate Expression', *The Jurist* (2004).

Cusack, Barbara Anne, 'The Diocesan Synod: A Teachable Moment in the Life of the Local Church', *The Jurist*, 63 (2003): 70–84.

Duffy, Eugene, 'Episcopal Conferences in the Context of Communion: Some Notes on the American Experience', *The Jurist*, 64 (2004): 137–67.

'Editorial' in *L'Osservatore Romano*, 26–7 January 2009.

Gallagher, Clarence, 'Collegiality in the East and the West in the First Millennium. A Study Based on the Canonical Collections', *The Jurist*, 64 (2004): 64–81.

Gauthier, Albert, 'Juridical Persons in the Code of Canon Law', *Studia Canonica* 25 (1991): 81–4.

Ghirlanda, Gianfranco, 'De Episcoporum Conferentia Deque Exercitio Potestatis Magisterii', *Periodica* 76 (1987).
— 'Doveri E Diritti Dei Fedeli Nella Communione Ecclesiale', *La Civilita Cattolica* 136, no. 1 (1985).

Green, Thomas J., 'Collegiality in the Church: Theology and Canon Law: Editor's Introduction', *The Jurist*, 64 (2004), no. 1: 1–5.

Grotaers, Jan, 'Collegiality put to the Test', *Concilium* 4 (1990).

Gröte, Heiner, 'The Catholic Conception of Collegiality from a European Reformed Perspective', *Concilium* 4, (1990): 54–63.

Hamer, Jerome, 'Les Conférence Épiscopales, Exércise De La Collégialité', *Nouvelle Théologique* 85 (1963).

Ivereigh, Austin, 'Through the Vatican White Smoke', *Open Democracy*, 4 April 2005.

König, Cardinal, 'My Vision for the Church of the Future', *The Tablet*, 27 March 1999.

Küng, Hans 'The Pope's Contradictions' in *Der Spiegel*, 25 March 2005, English translation in www.spiegel.de/international/spiegel/0,1518,348471,00.html. [Accessed 10.1.2009.]

Lash, Nicholas, 'Could the Shutters yet Come Down?', *The Tablet*, 24 January 2009, 13.

Pabel, Hilmar M. 'Vatican Counsel', *The Tablet*, 21 February 2009, 10–11.

Politi, Marco, 'The Churchs New Age of Dissent', *The Tablet*, 21 March 2009.

Tavard, George H., 'Collegiality According to Vatican II', *The Jurist*, 64 (2004): 82–115.

Wijlens, Mariam, 'Bishops and Their Relationship to a Local Church: A Canonical Perspective', *The Jurist*, 66 (2006): 211–41.

— 'Structures for Episcopal Leadership for Europe', *The Jurist* (2001): 190–212.

— 'Exercising Collegiality in a Supranational or Continental Institution Such as the FABC, CCEE and COMECE', *The Jurist*, 64 (2004): 168–204.

Willey, David. 'A Gaffe Too Far', *The Tablet*, 7 February 2009.